Reformed Church in America

**The Liturgy of the Reformed Church in America**

Reformed Church in America

**The Liturgy of the Reformed Church in America**

ISBN/EAN: 9783337260323

Printed in Europe, USA, Canada, Australia, Japan

Cover: Foto ©Lupo / pixelio.de

More available books at **www.hansebooks.com**

# THE LITURGY

OF THE

# REFORMED CHURCH IN AMERICA,

AS REPORTED TO THE

# GENERAL SYNOD OF 1873,

BY THE

*COMMITTEE ON REVISION.*

NEW YORK:
BOARD OF PUBLICATION R. C. A.,
34 VESEY STREET.
1873.

EDWARD O. JENKINS,
*PRINTER AND STEREOTYPER,*
20 North William Street, N. Y

# CONTENTS.

| | |
|---|---|
| I. ORDER OF SCRIPTURE LESSONS . . . | 6 |
| II. ORDER OF PUBLIC WORSHIP . . . | 9 |
|    I. Morning. | |
|    II. Evening. | |
| III. HOLY BAPTISM . . . . . | 23 |
|    I. Infants. | |
|    II. Adults. | |
| IV. RECEPTION OF BAPTIZED CHILDREN . . | 32 |
| V. THE LORD'S SUPPER . . . . . | 35 |
|    I. Preparatory. | |
|    II. Administration. | |
|    III. Thanksgiving. | |
| VI. CHURCH DISCIPLINE . . . | 47 |
|    I. Excommunication. | |
|    II. Re-admission. | |
| VII. ORDINATION . . . . . . | 56 |
|    I. Ministers. | |
|    II. Elders and Deacons. | |

|       |                              |       |
|-------|------------------------------|-------|
| VIII. | Installation of Ministers    | 73    |
| IX.   | Laying of Corner Stone       | 80    |
| X.    | Dedication                   | 85    |
| XI.   | Confirmation of Marriage     | 91    |
| XII.  | Burial of the Dead           | 95    |
| XIII. | Prayers for Special Occasions| 104   |
| XIV.  | The Creeds                   | 124   |

# THE LITURGY

## OF THE

# REFORMED CHURCH IN AMERICA.

**REVISED AND REPORTED TO THE GENERAL SYNOD OF 1873.**

---

### NOTE.

THIS Revised Liturgy is set forth as a general expression of the way in which the public services of religion should be performed. It is to be understood that it is not of binding authority, but is only recommended as containing suitable offices for public religious service. The only parts of our service which are obligatory, are those which are enjoined by the Constitution of the Church.

## ORDER OF SCRIPTURE LESSONS.

THE Synod of Dort, A.D., 1618, in its Rules of Church Government, [which "were recognized and expressly adopted" by the Reformed Dutch Church in America, in Convention, New York, October, A.D., 1771,] decreed as follows :

"Art. 67.—Besides the Sabbath day, the Churches shall likewise observe Christmas, Easter, and Whitsuntide, with the day succeeding each; and whereas, in most of the cities and provinces of the Netherlands, it is, moreover, customary to observe the day of the Circumcision and Ascension of our Lord, the Ministers where such practice has not been adopted, shall endeavor to prevail with the civil authority to establish a conformity with the other Churches."

This article bears witness to the ancient usage of our Church. The evident design of that usage was to bring into devout remembrance, year by year, the vital facts of the Advent, Death, and Resurrection of Our Blessed Lord, and of the Mission of the Holy Comforter. Thereto this Order of Scripture Lessons is adjusted, with the hope that if any, in the exercise of Christian liberty, shall use it, such use may be found to edification.

(LESSONS APPROPRIATE FOR PARTICULAR SEASONS.)

| | OLD TESTAMENT. | | NEW TESTAMENT. | |
|---|---|---|---|---|
| Humiliation | Isaiah, | 58 | Matthew, | 6:1-18 |
| or.. | Joel, | 2:1-18 | James, | 4 |
| Thanksgiving | Deut. | 16:1-17 | Philippians, | 4:4-30 |
| or.. | Isaiah, | 12 | Acts, | 17:24-31 |
| Holy Baptism | Isaiah, | 44:1-6 | Matthew, | 18:3-14 |
| or.. | Ezekiel, | 36:25-38 | Romans, | 6:3-14 |
| The Lord's Supper | Isaiah, | 53 | John, | 17 |
| or.. | " | 63:1-16 | Hebrews, | 10:1-23 |
| Ordination or Installation of a Minister. | " | 61 | 2 Timothy, | 4:1-8 |
| or.. | Ezekiel, | 38:1-20 | 1 Corinthians, | 13 |
| Ordination of Elders and Deacons | Isaiah, | 62 | Ephesians, | 4:1-16 |
| Dedication of a House of Worship | Exodus, | 40:17-38 | 1 Kings, | 9:1-9 |
| or.. | Hebrews, | 13:10-21 | Rev. | 21:10-27 |

# ORDER OF SCRIPTURE LESSONS

*FOR USE IN PUBLIC WORSHIP ON THE LORD'S DAY.*

## I.

### SEASON OF THE ADVENT OF OUR LORD.

#### (CHRISTMAS.)

The Order of Lessons for the Christmas Season begins with the fourth Sunday before Christmas.

| DAY. | MORNING. | | EVENING. | |
|---|---|---|---|---|
| | OLD TEST. | NEW TEST. | OLD TEST. | NEW TEST. |
| 4 Sun. before Christmas | Isaiah, 1 | Luke, 1:1-38 | Isaiah, 2 | Romans, 10 |
| 3 " | " 5 | " 1:39-56 | Malachi, 3 | " 12 |
| 2 " | " 25 | " 3:1-18 | Isaiah, 28:1-22 | " 14 |
| 1 " | " 30 | Matt., 3:1-12 | " 32 | 1 Corinth, 1 |
| Christmas (Dec. 25) | " 60 | Luke, 2:7-20 | " 9:1-7 | John 1:1-14 |
| Circumcision (Jan 1) | Gen. 17:1-10 | " 2:21-24 | Deut, 10:12-22 | Coloss., 2 |
| 1 Sun. after Christmas | Isaiah, 35 | " 2:25-52 | Isaiah, 40 | 1 Cor., 2 |
| 2 " | " 41 | Matt., 2:1-12 | " 42 | Heb., 2 |
| 3 " | " 44 | Mark, 1:1-15 | " 45 | 1 Cor. 3 |
| 4 " | " 51 | John, 1:15-28 | " 52:1-12 | " 13 |
| 5 " | " 54 | Matt., 4:1-11 | " 55 | 2 Cor., 4 |
| 6 " | " 57 | Luke, 4:14-32 | " 59 | " 5 |
| 7 " | " 61 | Matt., 5 | " 62 | Galat., 2 |
| 8 " | " 65 | " 6 | " 66 | " 3 |

The Lessons for the Sundays after Christmas are intended to be used until the 9th Sunday before Easter, and not further.

## II.

### SEASON OF THE DEATH AND RESURRECTION OF OUR LORD.

#### (EASTER.)

The Order of Lessons for the Easter Season begins with the 9th Sunday before Easter. Easter Sunday, corresponding to the time of the Jewish Passover, is the Sunday next after the full moon that follows the 21st of March; and if the full moon happen on a Sunday, it is the Sunday after. Ascension Day is forty days after Easter.

| DAY. | MORNING. | | EVENING. | |
|---|---|---|---|---|
| | OLD TEST. | NEW TEST. | OLD TEST. | NEW TEST. |
| 9 Sunday before Easter | Jerem., 5 | Matt., 7 | Jerem, 22 | Ephesians, 1 |
| 8 " | " 25 | Luke, 7:1-18 | " 36 | " 2 |
| 7 " | Lam., 1 | Mark, 6:1-29 | Lam, 3:1-36 | " 3 |
| 6 " | Jerem., 7 | Matt. 10 | Jerem., 9 | " 4 |
| 5 " | Ezek. 14 | Luke, 10:1-24 | Ezek.. 18 | " 5 |
| 4 " | " 20:1-26 | Mark, 9:1-29 | " 20:27-49 | " 6 |
| 3 " | Micah, 6 | Luke, 19:1-27 | Habakk, 3 | Philippians, 1 |
| 2 " | Haggai, 2:1-9 | " 21 | Zech. 13 | " 3 |
| 1 " | Dan., 9:4-27 | " 19:29-48 | Malachi, 4 | Hebrews, 5 |
| Good Friday | Gen., 22:1-19 | John, 19 | Isaiah, 53 | Philippians, 2 |
| EASTER | Exod 12:1-36 | " 20 | " 25 | Romans, 6 |
| 1 Sunday after Easter | Isaiah, 43 | Acts, 1 | " 48 | 1 Cor., 15:1-28 |
| 2 " | Hosea, 13 | " 3 | Hosea 14 | Colossians, 1 |
| 3 " | Joel. 8:1-8 | " 5:17-42 | Micah, 4 | " 8 |
| 4 " | Micah, 5 | " 6 | Nahum, 1 | 1 Thess., 3 |
| 5 " | Zech., 8 | " 8:14-40 | Zech., 10 | " 4 |
| Ascension | Deut., 10 | Luke, 24:44-53 | 2 Kings, 2 | Eph., 4:1-6 |

### III.
## SEASON OF THE MISSION OF THE HOLY COMFORTER.
#### (PENTECOST OR WHITSUNTIDE.)

The Order of Lessons for the Season of Pentecost begins with the Sunday before Pentecost. Pentecost, or Whitsuntide, is the seventh Sunday after Easter.

| DAY. | MORNING. | | EVENING. | |
|---|---|---|---|---|
| | OLD TEST. | NEW TEST. | OLD TEST. | NEW TEST. |
| 1 Sund. bef'e Pentecost | Joel, 2 | John, 17 | Zeph., 3 | 2 Thess., 8 |
| PENTECOST | Deut., 16:1 17 | Acts, 2:1-36 | Isaiah, 11 | Acts, 4:1-31 |
| Pentecost 1 Sund. after | Genesis, 1 | Matt., 3:10-17 | Genesis, 2 | 1 John, 5 |
| " 2 | " 3 | Acts, 9:1-31 | " 6 | 1 Tim., 6 |
| " 3 | " 9:1-19 | " 10 | " 15 | 2 Tim., 2 |
| " 4 | " 37 | " 11 | " 42 | " 3 |
| " 5 | " 43 | " 14 | " 45 | Titus, 2 |
| " 6 | " 49 | " 15 | " 50 | Hebrews, 10 |
| " 7 | Exodus 3 | " 17 | Exodus, 5 | " 11 |
| " 8 | " 9 | " 20 | " 10 | " 12 |
| " 9 | " 14 | " 24 | " 15 | " 13 |
| " 10 | Numb., 16 | " 26 | Numb., 22 | James, 1 |
| " 11 | " 23 | " 28 | " 24 | " 2 |
| " 12 | Deut., 4:1-40 | Matt., 18 | Deut., 5 | " 3 |
| " 13 | " 6 | " 20 | " 7 | " 4 |
| " 14 | " 8 | " 23 | " 9 | " 5 |
| " 15 | " 33 | " 25 | " 34 | 1 Peter, 1 |
| " 16 | Joshua, 23 | Mark, 4 | Joshua, 24 | " 2 |
| " 17 | Judges, 4 | " 13 | Judges, 5 | " 3 |
| " 18 | 1 Sam., 12 | Luke, 13 | 1 Sam'l, 17 | " 4 |
| " 19 | 2 Sam., 12 | " 15 | 2 Sam'l, 19 | " 5 |
| " 20 | 1 Kings, 8:1-21 | " 20 | 1 K'gs, 8:22-53 | 2 Peter, 1 |
| " 21 | " 17 | John, 3 | " 18 | " 2 |
| " 22 | 2 Kings, 5 | " 7 | 2 Kings, 19 | " 3 |
| " 23 | Daniel, 6 | " 8 | Daniel, 7 | 1 John, 1 |
| " 24 | Proverbs,1 | " 9 | Prov. 2 | " 2 |
| " 25 | " 3 | " 10 | " 8 | " 3 |
| " 26 | " 11 | " 11 | " 12 | Jude, |
| " 27 | " 13 | " 15 | " 14 | Rev. 1 |
| " 28 | " 15 | " 16 | " 16 | " 22 |

The Lessons for the Sundays after Pentecost are to be used until the fourth Sunday before Christmas, and no further.

# ORDER OF PUBLIC WORSHIP.

## Lord's Day Morning.

### I.

### INVOCATION.

*After a space for private devotion, the Minister shall introduce the public worship by invoking the Divine presence and blessing: The people uniting audibly in the Lord's Prayer and in the Amen at the close of every prayer in the public worship.*

ALMIGHTY GOD, unto whom all hearts are open, all desires known, and from whom no secrets are hid; cleanse the thoughts of our hearts by the inspiration of Thy Holy Spirit, that, we may perfectly love Thee and worthily magnify Thy Holy Name; through Jesus Christ our Lord: Who hath taught us when we pray to say:·

OUR FATHER WHO ART IN HEAVEN, HALLOWED BE THY NAME: THY KINGDOM COME: THY WILL BE DONE ON EARTH AS IT IS IN HEAVEN: GIVE US THIS DAY OUR DAILY BREAD: AND FOR-

GIVE US OUR DEBTS, AS WE FORGIVE OUR DEBTORS: AND LEAD US NOT INTO TEMPTATION, BUT DELIVER US FROM EVIL: FOR THINE IS THE KINGDOM, AND THE POWER, AND THE GLORY, FOR EVER. AMEN.

## II.
## SALUTATION.

THE peace of God which passeth all understanding keep your hearts and minds through Christ Jesus. AMEN.

*Or this:*

Grace be unto you, and peace from God our Father and from the Lord Jesus Christ. AMEN.

*Or this:*

The grace of our Lord Jesus Christ be with you all. AMEN.

*Or this:*

The Lord be with you.
*People.* And with thy spirit.

## III.
## READING OF SCRIPTURE.

### I.—THE TEN COMMANDMENTS.

Hear the law of God as it is written in the 20th chapter of the Book of Exodus.

GOD spake all these words, saying, I am the Lord

thy God, which have brought thee out of the land of Egypt, out of the house of bondage.

### I.

Thou shalt have no other gods before Me.

### II.

Thou shalt not make unto thee any graven image, or any likeness of anything that is in heaven above, or that is in the earth beneath, or that is in the water under the earth: thou shalt not bow down thyself to them, nor serve them: for I the Lord thy God am a jealous God, visiting the iniquity of the fathers upon the children unto the third and fourth generation of them that hate Me; and showing mercy unto thousands of them that love Me, and keep My commandments.

### III.

Thou shalt not take the Name of the Lord thy God in vain; for the Lord will not hold him guiltless that taketh His Name in vain.

### IV.

Remember the Sabbath-day to keep it holy. Six days shalt thou labor, and do all thy work: but the seventh day is the Sabbath of the Lord thy God: in it thou shalt not do any work, thou, nor thy son, nor thy daughter, thy man-servant, nor thy maid-servant, nor thy cattle, nor the stranger that is within thy gates: for in six days the Lord made heaven and earth, the sea, and all that in them is, and rested, the seventh day: wherefore, the Lord blessed the Sabbath-day, and hallowed it.

### V.

Honor thy father and thy mother: that thy days may be long upon the land which the Lord thy God giveth thee.

### VI.

Thou shalt not kill.

### VII.

Thou shalt not commit adultery.

### VIII.

Thou shalt not steal.

### IX.

Thou shalt not bear false witness against thy neighbor.

### X.

Thou shalt not covet thy neighbor's house, thou shalt not covet thy neighbor's wife, nor his man-servant, nor his maid-servant, nor his ox, nor his ass, nor anything that is thy neighbor's.

**Hear also what our Lord Jesus Christ saith.**

(ST. MATTHEW xxii. 37-40.)

Thou shalt love the Lord thy God with all thy heart, and with all thy soul, and with all thy mind. This is the first and great commandment. And the second is like unto it, Thou shalt love thy neighbor as thyself. On these two commandments hang all the law and the prophets.

Then may be sung the following response:

I.

LORD have mercy upon us, and write all these Thy laws in our hearts, we beseech Thee.  AMEN.

Or this:  II.

Thy word is a lamp unto my feet;
And a light unto my path.
How sweet are Thy words unto my taste;
Yea, sweeter than honey to my mouth.
Give me understanding, and I will keep Thy law.
For therein do I delight, O Lord my God.
AMEN.

LESSON.

II.—FROM THE OLD TESTAMENT.

LESSON.

III.—FROM THE NEW TESTAMENT.

After either or both of which may be sung a GLORIA or any suitable Chant.

IV.

SINGING.

V.

PRAYER.

Which will ordinarily be free. But if desirable, the following Litany, which is a literal translation from the Reformer Bucer's "Reformation of Doctrine and Worship," may be used: The People repeating audibly the responses, which are printed in small capitals.

## THE LITANY.

O GOD the Father of Heaven, have mercy upon us.

O God the Son, Redeemer of the world, have have mercy upon us.

O God the Holy Ghost, HAVE MERCY UPON US.

Be merciful unto us, and spare us, O Lord.

Be merciful unto us, and deliver us, O Lord.

From all sin, from all error, from all evil, from the wiles of the devil, deliver us, O Lord.

From dying suddenly and unprepared; from pestilence and famine, from war and slaughter, from sedition and conspiracy, from lightning and tempest, from everlasting death, deliver us, O Lord.

By the mystery of Thy holy Incarnation, by Thy holy Nativity, by Thy Baptism, Fasting, and Temptations, deliver us, O Lord.

By Thine Agony and bloody Sweat, by Thy Cross and Passion, by Thy Death and Burial, by Thy Resurrection and Ascension, by the coming of the Holy Ghost the Comforter, deliver us, O Lord.

In all time of our tribulation, in all time of our felicity, in the hour of death, in the day of judgment, DELIVER US, O LORD.

We sinners beseech Thee to hear us:

That it may please Thee to rule and govern Thy Holy Church Universal.

That it may please Thee to preserve in soundness of word and holiness of life, all pastors and ministers of Thy Church.

That it may please Thee to remove all sects and scandals.

That it may please Thee to bring back into the way of truth all such as wander and have been led astray.

That it may please Thee to crush Satan under our feet.

That it may please Thee to send forth faithful laborers into Thy harvest.

That it may please Thee to grant the increase of Thy Word and the fruit of Thy Spirit unto all that hear.

That it may please Thee to raise the fallen, and strengthen those that stand.

That it may please Thee to console the weak-hearted, and succor the tempted.

That it may please Thee to give peace and concord unto all rulers and governors.

That it may please Thee to guide and protect our Chief Magistrate, with all his counsellors.

That it may please Thee to bless and preserve our people, and all in authority among us.

That it may please Thee to look upon the afflicted, and those that are in danger; and to comfort them.

That it may please Thee to succor all women in the perils of child-birth.

That it may please Thee to cherish and protect young children and sick persons.

That it may please Thee to defend and suitably provide for the orphans and widows.

That it may please Thee to grant freedom unto captives.

That it may please Thee to have mercy upon all men.

That it may please Thee to forgive our enemies, persecutors, and slanderers, and to convert them.

That it may please Thee to give and preserve the fruits of the earth.

That it may please Thee to grant all these our requests.

WE BESEECH THEE TO HEAR US.

Lamb of God, who takest away the sin of the world, HAVE MERCY UPON US.

Lamb of God, who takest away the sin of the world, GRANT US THY PEACE.

Lord, deal not with us after our sins, neither reward us according to our iniquities.

O God, Merciful Father, who despisest not the groans of the contrite, nor rejectest the desire of the sorrowful: be favorable to our prayers, which, in our afflictions that continually oppress us, we pour out before Thee; and graciously hear them; that those things which the craft of the devil or of man worketh against us, may be brought to naught, and by the counsel of Thy goodness be scattered; that being hurt by no persecutions, we may ever give thanks unto Thee in Thy holy Church: through Jesus Christ our Lord.

O God, from whom all holy desires, all good counsels, and all just works proceed: Give unto Thy servants that peace which the world cannot give; that both our hearts may be set to obey Thy commandments, and also that we, being defended from the fear of our enemies, may by Thy protection pass our time in rest and quietness: Through Jesus Christ our Lord. AMEN.

### VI.

## SINGING.

### VII.

## SERMON.

### VIII.

## THANK-OFFERING OF ALMS.

### IX.

## SINGING,

### With Doxology.

### X.

## PRAYER.

If desirable, in the use of any of the following:

GRANT, we beseech Thee, Almighty God, that the words which we have heard this day with our outward ears, may, through Thy grace, be so grafted inwardly in our hearts, that they may bring forth in us the fruit of good living; to the honor and praise of Thy Name: Through Jesus Christ our Lord. AMEN.

O GOD, Holy Ghost, Sanctifier of the Faithful, visit, we pray Thee, this congregation with Thy love and favor; enlighten their minds more and more with the light of the everlasting Gospel; graft in their hearts a love of the truth; increase in them true religion; nourish them with all goodness; and of Thy great mercy keep them in the same, O Blessed Spirit: Whom, with the Father and the Son, together, we worship and glorify as one God, world without end. AMEN.

O ALMIGHTY GOD! who alone canst order the unruly wills and affections of sinful men: Grant unto us Thy people, that we may love the things which Thou commandest, and desire that which Thou dost promise; that so, among the sundry and manifold changes of the world, our hearts may surely there be fixed, where true joys are to be found: Through Jesus Christ our Lord. AMEN.

ALMIGHTY GOD, who hast given us grace at this time with one accord to make our common supplications unto Thee, and dost promise that when two or three are gathered together in Thy Name, Thou wilt grant their requests: Fulfil now, O Lord, the desires and petitions of thy servants, as may be most expedient for them; granting us in this world knowledge of Thy truth, and in the world to come life everlasting. AMEN.

## XI.
## BENEDICTION.

# ORDER OF PUBLIC WORSHIP.

## Lord's Day Evening.

### I.

### INVOCATION.

After a space for private devotion, the Minister shall introduce the public worship by invoking the Divine presence and blessing: The people uniting audibly in the Lord's Prayer and in the Amen at the close of every prayer in the public worship.

DIRECT us, O Lord, in all our doings, with Thy most gracious favor, and further us with Thy continual help; that in all our works, begun, continued, and ended in Thee, we may glorify Thy holy Name; and, finally, by Thy mercy, obtain everlasting life; through Jesus Christ our Lord. Who hath taught us to pray after this manner:

OUR FATHER WHO ART IN HEAVEN, HALLOWED BE THY NAME: THY KINGDOM COME: THY WILL BE DONE ON EARTH AS IT IS IN HEAVEN: GIVE US THIS DAY OUR DAILY BREAD: AND FOR-

GIVE US OUR DEBTS, AS WE FORGIVE OUR DEBTORS: AND LEAD US NOT INTO TEMPTATION, BUT DELIVER US FROM EVIL: FOR THINE IS THE KINGDOM, AND THE POWER, AND THE GLORY, FOR EVER. AMEN.

## II.
## SALUTATION.

THE peace of God, which passeth all understanding, keep your hearts and minds, through Christ Jesus. AMEN.

*Or this:*

Grace be unto you, and peace from God our Father and from the Lord Jesus Christ. AMEN.

*Or this:*

The Lord be with you.
*People.* And with thy spirit.

## III.
## SCRIPTURE LESSONS.

I.—FROM THE OLD TESTAMENT.

II.—FROM THE NEW TESTAMENT.

After either or both of which may be sung a GLORIA, or any other suitable chant.

## IV.
## SINGING.

## V.

## THE APOSTLES' CREED.

*The People standing and repeating audibly with the Minister.*

I BELIEVE IN GOD THE FATHER ALMIGHTY, MAKER OF HEAVEN AND EARTH.

AND IN JESUS CHRIST, HIS ONLY SON, OUR LORD; WHO WAS CONCEIVED BY THE HOLY GHOST; BORN OF THE VIRGIN MARY, SUFFERED UNDER PONTIUS PILATE; WAS CRUCIFIED, DEAD AND BURIED; HE DESCENDED INTO HELL: THE THIRD DAY HE ROSE AGAIN FROM THE DEAD; HE ASCENDED INTO HEAVEN, AND SITTETH AT THE RIGHT HAND OF GOD THE FATHER ALMIGHTY: FROM THENCE HE SHALL COME TO JUDGE THE QUICK AND THE DEAD.

I BELIEVE IN THE HOLY GHOST; THE HOLY CATHOLIC CHURCH, THE COMMUNION OF SAINTS; THE FORGIVENESS OF SINS; THE RESURRECTION OF THE BODY; AND THE LIFE EVERLASTING. AMEN.

## VI.

## PRAYER.

*Which will ordinarily be free, but if desirable, the Litany may at any time be used as in the Morning Service.*

## VII.

## SINGING.

## VIII.

## SERMON.

## IX.

## THANK-OFFERING OF ALMS.

## X.

## SINGING, WITH DOXOLOGY.

## XI.

## PRAYER.

*If desirable, in the use of either of the following:*

GRANT, we beseech Thee, Almighty God, that the words which we have heard this day with our outward ears, may, through Thy grace, be so grafted inwardly in our hearts, that they may bring forth in us the fruit of good living; to the honor and praise of Thy Name: Through Jesus Christ our Lord. AMEN.

O GOD, Holy Ghost, Sanctifier of the Faithful, visit, we pray Thee, this congregation with Thy love and favor; enlighten their minds more and more with the light of the everlasting Gospel; graft in their hearts a love of the truth; increase in them true religion; nourish them with all goodness; and of Thy great mercy keep them in the same, O Blessed Spirit: Whom, with the Father and the Son, together, we worship and glorify as one God, world without end. AMEN.

## XII.

## BENEDICTION.

# THE SACRAMENTS.

## III.

### The Office for the Administration of Holy Baptism.*

THE principal parts of the *doctrine* of Holy Baptism are these three:

*First.* That we with our children are conceived and born in sin, and therefore [are children of wrath, insomuch that we] cannot enter into the Kingdom of God, except we are born again. [This, the dipping in or sprinkling with water teaches us, whereby the impurity of our souls is signified, and we are admonished to loathe and humble ourselves before God, and seek for our purification and salvation without ourselves.]

*Secondly.* Holy Baptism witnesseth and sealeth unto us the washing away of our sins, through Jesus Christ. Therefore we are baptized IN THE NAME OF THE FATHER, AND OF THE SON, AND OF THE HOLY GHOST. [For when we are baptized in the name of the FATHER, God the Father witnesseth and sealeth unto us, that He doth make an eternal covenant of grace with us, and adopts us for His children and heirs, and therefore will provide us with every good thing, and avert all evil or turn it to our profit. And when we are baptized in the name of the

---
\* The abbreviations in this Office may be used at the option of the Minister.

Son, the Son sealeth unto us that He doth wash us in His blood from all our sins, incorporating us into the fellowship of His death and resurrection, so that we are freed from all our sins and accounted righteous before God. In like manner, when we are baptized in the name of the Holy Ghost, the Holy Ghost assures us, by this Holy Sacrament, that He will dwell in us, and sanctify us to be members of Christ, applying unto us that which we have in Christ, namely, the washing away of our sins and the daily renewing of our lives, till we shall finally be presented without spot or wrinkle among the assembly of the elect in life eternal.]

*Thirdly.* Whereas in all covenants there are contained two parts, therefore are we by God, through Baptism, admonished of, and obliged unto new obedience, namely, that we cleave to this One God, Father, Son, and Holy Ghost; that we trust in Him and love Him with all our heart, with all our soul, with all our mind, and with all our strength; that we forsake the world, crucify our old nature, and walk in a new and holy life.

And if we sometimes, through weakness, fall into sin, we must not therefore despair of God's mercy, nor continue in sin, since Baptism is a seal and undoubted testimony that we have an eternal covenant of grace with God.

### I.

#### TO INFANTS OF BELIEVERS.

And although our young children do not understand these things, we may not therefore exclude them from Baptism; for as they are, without their knowledge, partakers of the condemnation in Adam, so are they again received unto grace in Christ;

as God speaketh unto Abraham, the father of all the faithful, and therefore unto us and our children, (Gen. 17:7,) saying: " I will establish My covenant between Me and thee, and thy seed after thee, in their generations, for an everlasting covenant; to be a God unto thee, and to thy seed after thee." This also the Apostle Peter testifieth, with these words, (Acts 2:39:) " For the promise is unto you, and to your children, and to all that are afar off, even as many as the Lord our God shall call." Therefore God formerly commanded them to be circumcised, which was a seal of the Covenant, and of the righteousness of faith; and therefore Christ also embraced them, laid His hands upon them and blessed them. (Mark 10:16.)

Since then Baptism is come in the place of circumcision, infants are to be baptized as heirs of the Kingdom of God and of His Covenant. And parents are in duty bound, further to instruct their children herein, when they shall arrive at years of discretion.

That therefore this Holy Ordinance of God may be administered to His glory, to our comfort, and to the edification of His Church, let us call upon His holy Name.

PRAYER.

O Almighty and Eternal God, we beseech Thee that Thou wilt be pleased of Thine infinite mercy, graciously to look upon *these children*, and incorporate *them* by Thy Holy Spirit into Thy Son Jesus Christ, that *they* may be buried with Him into His death and be raised with Him in newness of life; that *they* may daily follow Him, joyfully bearing *their* cross, and cleave unto Him in true faith, firm hope, and ardent love; that *they* may, with a comfortable sense of Thy favor, leave this life, which is nothing but a continual death, and at the last day, may appear without terror before the judgment-seat of Christ Thy Son, through Jesus Christ our Lord, who with Thee and the Holy Ghost, One Only God, lives and reigns forever. AMEN.

AN EXHORTATION TO THE PARENTS, AND THOSE WHO COME WITH THEM TO BAPTISM.

Beloved in the Lord Jesus Christ, you have heard that Baptism is an Ordinance of God, to seal unto us and to our seed His Covenant. Therefore it must be used for that end, and not out of custom or superstition. That it may then be manifest that you are thus minded, you are to answer sincerely to these questions:

*First.* Do you acknowledge, that although our children are conceived and born in sin, and therefore are subject to all miseries, yea, to condemnation itself; yet that they are sanctified* in Christ, and therefore, as members of His Church, ought to be baptized?

*Secondly.* Do you acknowledge the doctrine which is contained in the Old and New Testament, and in the Articles of the Christian faith, and which is taught here in this Christian Church, to be the true and perfect† doctrine of salvation?

---

\* "My children:" Ezek. 16:21.   "They are holy:" 1 Cor. 7:14.
† *Dutch*: Volkomene—complete.

*Thirdly.* Do you promise and intend to see *these children*, when come to the years of discretion, instructed and brought up in the aforesaid doctrine, or to help or cause *them* to be instructed therein, to the utmost of your power?
*Answer.* Yes.

Then the Minister of God's Word, in baptizing, shall say:

——————, I baptize thee, in the name of the Father, and of the Son, and of the Holy Ghost. AMEN.

### THANKSGIVING.

Almighty God and Merciful Father, we thank and praise Thee, that Thou hast forgiven us, and our children, all our sins, through the blood of Thy Beloved Son Jesus Christ, and received us through Thy Holy Spirit, as members of Thy Only Begotten Son, and adopted us to be Thy children, and sealed and confirmed the same unto us by Holy Baptism. We beseech Thee, through the same Son of Thy love, that Thou wilt be pleased always to govern *these* baptized *children* by Thy Holy Spirit; that *they* may be piously and religiously educated, increase and grow up in the Lord Jesus Christ; that *they* then may acknowledge Thy Fatherly goodness and mercy, which Thou hast shown to *them* and us; and live in all righteousness, under our only Teacher, King, and High-Priest, Jesus Christ; and manfully fight against and overcome sin, the devil, and his whole dominion, to the end that *they* may eternally praise and magnify Thee, and Thy Son Jesus Christ, together with the Holy Ghost, the One Only True God. AMEN.

## II.

### TO ADULT PERSONS.

However, children of Christian parents, although they understand not this mystery, must be baptized, by virtue of the Covenant; yet it is not lawful to baptize those who have come to years of discretion, except they first be sensible of their sins, and make confession both of their repentance and their faith in Christ. For this cause [not only did John the Baptist preach, according to the command of God, the baptism of repentance, and baptize for the remission of sin, those who confessed their sins, (Mark 1 : 4;) but] our Lord Jesus Christ [also] commanded His disciples to teach all nations, and then to baptize them, in the name of the Father, and of the Son, and of the Holy Ghost, adding this promise: "He that believeth and is baptized shall be saved." According to which rule the Apostles [Acts 2, 10, 16] baptized none who were of years of discretion, but such as made confession of their faith and repentance. Therefore it is not lawful now to baptize any other adult persons, than such as have been taught the mysteries of Holy Baptism by the preaching of the Gospel, and are able to give an account of their faith by the confession of the mouth.

Since therefore you, ―――――, are also desirous of Holy Baptism, to the end it may be to you a seal of your engrafting into the Church of God ; that it

may appear that you do not only receive the Christian religion,
[in which you have been privately instructed by us, and of which also you have made confession before us,]
but that you, through the grace of God, intend and purpose to lead a life according to the same; you are sincerely to give answer before God and His Church:

*First.* Dost thou believe in the Only True God, distinct in three persons, Father, Son, and Holy Ghost, Who hath made heaven and earth, and all that in them is, of nothing, and still maintains and governs them, insomuch that nothing comes to pass, either in heaven or on earth, without His divine will?

*Answer.* Yes.

*Secondly.* Dost thou believe that thou art conceived and born in sin, and therefore art a child of wrath by nature,
[wholly incapable of doing any good and prone to all evil;]
and that thou hast frequently, both in thought, word, and deed, transgressed the commandments of the Lord; and art thou heartily sorry for these sins?

*Answer.* Yes.

*Thirdly.* Dost thou believe that Christ, who is the True and Eternal God, and Very Man,
[who took His human nature on Him out of the flesh and blood of the Virgin Mary,]
is given thee of God, to be thy Saviour; and

that thou dost receive, by this faith, remission of sins in His blood; and that thou art made, by the power of the Holy Ghost, a member of Jesus Christ and of His Church?

*Answer.* Yes.

*Fourthly.* Dost thou assent to all the Articles of the Christian religion, as they are taught here in this Christian Church, according to the Word of God; and purpose steadfastly to continue in the same doctrine to the end of thy life; and also dost thou reject all heresies and schisms, repugnant to this doctrine, and promise to persevere in the communion of our Christian Church, not only in the hearing of the Word, but also in the use of the Lord's Supper?

*Answer.* Yes.

*Fifthly.* Hast thou taken a firm resolution always to lead a Christian life; to forsake the world and its evil lusts, as is becoming the members of Christ and His Church; and to submit thyself to all Christian admonitions?

*Answer.* Yes.

The Good and Great God mercifully grant His grace and blessing to this thy purpose, through Jesus Christ. AMEN.

<small>Then the Minister of God's Word, in baptizing, shall say:</small>

—————, I baptize thee, in the name of the Father, and of the Son, and of the Holy Ghost. AMEN.

### THANKSGIVING.

Almighty God, our Heavenly Father, we give Thee most humble and hearty thanks that Thou hast called us to the knowledge of Thy grace, and unto the faith of Thy Son, and unto the Covenant of salvation, wherein we are sealed by Holy Baptism. Give Thy Holy Spirit to these Thy servants, that, being born again and made heirs of God, they may keep themselves in Thy love, and receive the fulfilment of Thy promises; through our Lord Jesus Christ, Who, with Thee, O Father, and the Holy Ghost, the One Only True God, liveth and reigneth, world without end. AMEN.

# IV.

## The Public Reception into Full Communion of those who have been Baptized in Infancy.

*The Candidates shall stand before the Minister. While they are coming forward, an appropriate hymn may be sung.*

*Then the Minister will say:*

DEARLY BELOVED IN CHRIST. As *children* of your Heavenly Father you stand here for the deliberate and public ratification in your own *persons* of that Covenant of God of which your Baptism is the seal. You have already been duly instructed, and have made confession before us of your faith in the Blessed Saviour. And now in this most solemn manner, before God and His Church, you are to repeat and renew that confession.

I ask *each one* of you, then:

*First*. Dost thou believe in God the Father Almighty, Maker of heaven and earth?

*Answer*. I do.

*Secondly*. Dost thou believe in Jesus Christ His only Son, our Lord, who was conceived by the Holy Ghost, born of the Virgin Mary, suffered under Pontius Pilate, was crucified, dead and buried; He descended into hell; the third day He rose again from the dead; He ascended into heaven, and sitteth at the right hand of God the Father Almighty; from thence He shall come to judge the quick and the dead?

*Answer.* I do.

*Thirdly.* Dost thou believe in the Holy Ghost; the Holy Catholic Church, the communion of saints; the forgiveness of sins; the resurrection of the body; and the life everlasting?

*Answer.* I do.

*Fourthly.* Dost thou purpose steadfastly to continue to the end of thy life in the truth affirmed in these Articles of the Christian Faith as they are taught here in this Church, according to the Word of God, rejecting all heresies and schisms repugnant thereto?

*Answer.* I do.

*Fifthly.* Dost thou promise to persevere in the communion of the Christian Church, and in the diligent use of all the means of grace, especially in the hearing of the Word and the use of the Lord's Supper, to seek the things that make for purity and peace, and to submit thyself to all Christian care and admonition?

*Answer.* I do.

Then the Minister will say:

Since, then, *thou hast* witnessed this good confession; in the name of the Church and of Jesus Christ her Lord and Head, I do now welcome *thee* to full communion with the People of God.

[The following, or some other appropriate blessing, will then be used, given to each one separately, or to all together, as the Minister may choose.]

THE mountains shall depart and the hills be removed; but My kindness shall not depart from thee, neither shall the covenant of My peace be removed, saith the Lord that hath mercy on thee.

The LORD bless thee and keep thee!

The LORD make His face shine upon thee and be gracious unto thee!

The LORD lift up His countenance upon thee and give thee peace! AMEN.

[The Minister will then offer the following Thanksgiving.]

Almighty and Everlasting God, we thank and praise Thee that Thou hast vouchsafed unto *these* Thy *servants*, power and grace, to own and accept for *themselves* Thy holy covenant, sealed and confirmed to *them* in *their* baptism. Strengthen *them* we beseech Thee with the Holy Ghost the Comforter. Increase in *them* daily Thy manifold gifts of grace; the spirit of wisdom and understanding, the spirit of counsel and might, the spirit of knowledge and of the fear of the Lord. Keep *them* from the evil that is in the world. Defend *them* from the power of the devil. Enable *them* to walk in the Spirit, that *they* may not fulfil the lusts of the flesh; and so lead *them* in the knowledge and obedience of Thy Word that *they* may obtain everlasting life, through Jesus Christ our Lord, Who, with Thee and the Holy Ghost, liveth and reigneth, ever one God, world without end. AMEN.

# V.

## The Office for the Administration of the Lord's Supper.

---

### I.*

*Before the administration of the Holy Communion the Minister shall say :*

BELOVED in the Lord Jesus Christ, attend to the words of the institution of the Holy Supper of our Lord Jesus Christ, as they are delivered by the holy Apostle Paul, 1 Cor. xi : 23–30.

"For I have received of the Lord that which also I delivered unto you, That the Lord Jesus, the same night in which He was betrayed, took bread ; and when He had given thanks, He brake it, and said, Take, eat : this is My body, which is broken for you: this do in remembrance of Me. After the same manner, also, He took the cup when He had supped, saying, This cup is the new testament in My blood : this do ye, as oft as ye drink it, in remembrance of Me. For as often as ye eat this bread, and drink this cup, ye do show the Lord's

---

\* This first part of the Communion Office, being of its nature preparatory, may at the discretion of the Minister, be used at the usual service, preparatory to the Communion. The use of the abbreviations in this Office is at the option of the Minister.

death till He come. Wherefore, whosoever shall eat this bread, and drink this cup of the Lord unworthily, shall be guilty of the body and blood of the Lord. But let a man examine himself, and so let him eat of that bread and drink of that cup; for he that eateth and drinketh unworthily, eateth and drinketh damnation* to himself, not discerning the Lord's body."

That we may [now] celebrate the Supper of the Lord to our comfort, it is above all things necessary;

I. Rightly to examine ourselves.

II. To direct the Supper to that end for which Christ hath ordained and instituted the same, namely, to His remembrance.

The true EXAMINATION of ourselves consists of these three parts:

*First.* That every one consider by himself his sins and the curse due to him for them, to the end that he may abhor and humble himself before God: considering that the wrath of God against sin is so great, that, rather than it should go unpunished, He hath punished the same in His Beloved Son Jesus Christ, with the bitter and shameful death of the cross.

*Secondly.* That every one examine his own heart, whether he doth believe this faithful promise of God, that all his sins are forgiven him only for the sake of the passion and death of Jesus Christ; and that the perfect righteousness of Christ is imputed and freely given him as his own, yea, so perfectly

---

* Greek, K$\rho\iota\mu a$—Dutch, Oordeel. Eng., judgment, condemnation.

as if he had satisfied in his own person for all his sins, and fulfilled all righteousness.

*Thirdly.* That every one examine his own conscience, whether he purposeth henceforth to show true thankfulness to God in his whole life, and to walk uprightly before Him; as also, whether he hath laid aside unfeignedly, all enmity, hatred, and envy, and doth firmly resolve henceforth to walk in true love and peace with his neighbor.

All those, then, who are thus disposed, God will certainly receive in mercy, and count them worthy partakers of the table of His Son Jesus Christ. On the contrary, those who do not feel this testimony in their hearts, eat and drink judgment to themselves.

Therefore, we also, according to the command of Christ and the Apostle Paul, admonish all those [who are defiled with the following sins] to keep themselves from the table of the Lord, [and declare to them that they have no part of the kingdom of Christ; such as all idolaters; all those who invoke deceased saints, angels, or other creatures; all those who worship images; all enchanters, diviners, charmers, and those who confide in such enchantments; all despisers of God and His Word, and of the Holy Sacraments; all blasphemers; all those who are given to raise discord, sects, and mutiny, in church or state; all perjured persons; all those who are disobedient to their parents and superiors; all murderers, contentious persons, and those who live in hatred and envy against their neighbors; all adulterers, whoremongers, drunkards, thieves, usurers, robbers, gamesters, covetous; and all] who lead offensive lives.

All these, while they continue in such sins, shall abstain from this meat, which Christ hath ordained only for the faithful, lest their judgment and condemnation be made the heavier.

But this is not designed, dearly beloved brethren and sisters in the Lord, to deject the contrite hearts of the faithful, as if none might come to the Supper of the Lord, but those who are without sin. For we do not come to this Supper to testify thereby that we are perfect and righteous in ourselves; but on the contrary, considering that we seek our life out of ourselves, in Jesus Christ, we acknowledge that we lie in the midst of death. Therefore, notwithstanding we feel many infirmities and miseries in ourselves; as namely, that we have not perfect faith, and that we do not give ourselves to serve God with such zeal as we are bound, but have daily to strive with the weakness of our faith, and the evil lusts of our flesh; yet, since we are, by the grace of the Holy Ghost, sorry for these weaknesses, and earnestly desirous to fight against our unbelief, and to live according to all the commandments of God, therefore we rest assured that no sin or infirmity, which still remaineth, against our will, in us, can hinder us from being received of God in mercy, and from being made worthy partakers of this heavenly meat and drink.

## II.

*At the administration of the Holy Communion, the Minister shall say:*

BELOVED in the Lord Jesus Christ.

Let us now, [also,] consider to what end the Lord hath instituted His Supper, namely, that we do it in remembrance of Him. Now, after this manner are we to remember Him by it.

1. That we be confidently persuaded in our hearts, that our Lord Jesus Christ, according to the promises made to our forefathers in the Old Testament, was sent of the Father into the world: that He assumed our flesh and blood: that He bore for us the wrath of God, under which we should have perished everlastingly, from the beginning of His incarnation to the end of His life upon earth: that He fulfilled for us all obedience to the divine law, and righteousness, especially when the weight of our sins and the wrath of God pressed out of Him the bloody sweat in the garden, where He was bound that we might be freed from our sins: that He afterward suffered innumerable reproaches, that we might never be confounded; that He, although innocent, was condemned to death, that we might be acquitted at the judgment-seat of God: yea, that He suffered His blessed body to be nailed on the cross, that He might affix thereon the handwriting of our sins: that He also took upon Himself the curse due to us, that He might fill us with His blessings: that He humbled Himself unto the deepest reproach and pains of hell, both in body and soul, on the tree of the cross, when he cried out with a loud voice, *My God, My God! why hast*

*thou forsaken me?* that we might be accepted of God, and never be forsaken of Him: and finally that He confirmed, with His death and shedding of His blood, the new and eternal testament, that covenant of grace and reconciliation, when He said, *It is finished.*

2. And, that we might firmly believe that we belong to this Covenant of Grace, the Lord Jesus Christ, in His Last Supper, " took bread, and when He had given thanks, He brake it, and gave it to His disciples, and said, Take, eat, this is My body which is broken for you, this do in remembrance of Me: in like manner also, after supper, He took the cup, gave thanks and said, Drink ye all of it; this cup is the new testament in My blood, which is shed for you and for many, for the remission of sins; this do ye, as often as ye drink it, in remembrance of Me." That is, as often as ye eat of this bread, and drink of this cup, you shall thereby, as by a sure remembrance and pledge, be admonished and assured of this My hearty love and faithfulness toward you: that whereas you should otherwise have suffered eternal death, I have given My body to the death of the cross, and shed My blood for you; and as certainly feed and nourish your hungry and thirsty soul with My crucified body and shed blood to everlasting life, as this bread is broken before your eyes, and this cup is given to you, and you eat and drink the same with your mouth, in remembrance of Me.

From this institution of the Holy Supper of our Lord Jesus Christ, we see that He directs our faith and trust to His Perfect Sacrifice, once offered on the cross, as to the only ground and foundation of our salvation; wherein He is become to our hungry and thirsty souls, the true meat and drink of life eternal. For by His death He hath taken away the cause of our eternal death and misery, namely, sin; and obtained for us the Quickening Spirit, that we by the same, which dwelleth in Christ as the Head, and in us as His members, might have true communion with Him, and be made partakers of all His blessings, of life eternal, righteousness, and glory.

Besides, that we, by the same Spirit may also be united as members of one Body, in true brotherly love; as the holy Apostle saith, "For we, being many, are one bread and one body; for we are all partakers of that one bread."

[For as out of many grains one meal is ground and one bread baked, and out of many berries being pressed together, one wine floweth and mixeth itself together; so shall we all, who by a true faith are ingrafted into Christ, through brotherly love be altogether one body, for the sake of Christ, our Beloved Saviour, who hath so exceedingly loved us; and shall show this, not only in word, but also in very deed towards one another.]

Hereto assist us, the Almighty God and Father of our Lord Jesus Christ, through His Holy Spirit! AMEN.

That we may obtain all this, let us humble ourselves before God, and with true faith implore His grace.

## PRAYER.

O Most Merciful God and Father, we beseech Thee, that Thou wilt be pleased, in this Supper, in which we celebrate the glorious remembrance of the bitter death of Thy Beloved Son Jesus Christ, to work in our hearts through the Holy Spirit, that we may daily, more and more, with true confidence, give ourselves up unto Thy Son Jesus Christ, so that our afflicted and contrite hearts, through the power of the Holy Ghost, may be fed and comforted with His true body and blood; yea, with Him, True God and Man, that Only Heavenly Bread: and that we may no longer live in our sins, but He in us, and we in Him; and thus truly be made partakers of the new and everlasting testament and covenant of grace: that we may not doubt that Thou wilt for ever be our Gracious Father, never more imputing our sins unto us, and providing us, as Thy beloved children and heirs, with all things necessary, as well for the body as the soul. Grant us also Thy grace, that we may take upon us our cross cheerfully, deny ourselves, confess our Saviour, and in all tribulations, with uplifted heads expect our Lord Jesus Christ from heaven, where He will make our mortal bodies like unto His most glorious body, and take us unto Him in eternity.

OUR FATHER WHO ART IN HEAVEN, HALLOWED BE THY NAME: THY KINGDOM COME: THY WILL BE DONE ON EARTH AS IT IS IN HEAVEN: GIVE US THIS DAY OUR DAILY BREAD: AND FORGIVE US OUR DEBTS, AS WE FORGIVE OUR DEBTORS:

AND LEAD US NOT INTO TEMPTATION, BUT DELIVER US FROM EVIL: FOR THINE IS THE KINGDOM, AND THE POWER, AND THE GLORY, FOR EVER. AMEN.

Strengthen us also by this Holy Supper in the Catholic undoubted Christian Faith, whereof we make confession with our mouths and hearts, saying :*

I BELIEVE IN GOD, THE FATHER ALMIGHTY, MAKER OF HEAVEN AND EARTH; AND IN JESUS CHRIST HIS ONLY SON OUR LORD; WHO WAS CONCEIVED BY THE HOLY GHOST, BORN OF THE VIRGIN MARY, SUFFERED UNDER PONTIUS PILATE, WAS CRUCIFIED, DEAD AND BURIED; HE DESCENDED INTO HELL; THE THIRD DAY HE ROSE AGAIN FROM THE DEAD; HE ASCENDED INTO HEAVEN; AND SITTETH AT THE RIGHT HAND OF GOD THE FATHER ALMIGHTY; FROM THENCE HE SHALL COME TO JUDGE THE QUICK AND THE DEAD.

I BELIEVE IN THE HOLY GHOST; THE HOLY CATHOLIC CHURCH, THE COMMUNION OF SAINTS; THE FORGIVENESS OF SINS; THE RESURRECTION OF THE BODY; AND THE LIFE EVERLASTING. AMEN.

That we may be now fed with the True Heavenly Bread, Christ Jesus, let us not cleave with our hearts unto the external bread and wine, but lift them up on high in heaven, where Christ Jesus is our Advocate, at the right hand of His Heavenly Father, whither all the Articles of our Faith lead us; not

---

\* The words "*with our mouths and hearts*," evidently require the *audible* confession of these "Articles of the Christian Faith," both by the Minister and the people. And such was the ancient usage. It is recommended that it be restored.

doubting that, through the working of the Holy Ghost, we shall as certainly be fed and refreshed in our souls with His Body and Blood, as we receive the holy bread and wine, in remembrance of Him.

In breaking and distributing the bread, the Minister shall say:

The bread which we break, is the communion of the Body of Christ.

And when he giveth the cup:

The cup of blessing, which we bless, is the communion of the Blood of Christ.

During the Communion, a Psalm shall or may be devoutly sung, or some chapter read, in remembrance of the death of Christ, as Isaiah liii, John xiii, xiv, xv, xvi, xvii, xviii, or the like.

### III.

After the Communion, the Minister shall say:

BELOVED IN THE LORD, since the Lord hath now fed our souls at His table, let us therefore jointly praise His Holy Name, with thanksgiving, and every one say in his heart, thus:\*

Bless the Lord, O my soul; and all that is within me, bless His Holy Name.

BLESS THE LORD, O MY SOUL; AND FORGET NOT ALL HIS BENEFITS.

Who forgiveth all thine iniquities; Who healeth all thy diseases.

---

\* It is recommended that this Psalm of Thanksgiving, (Psalm 103), be read responsively by the Minister and people; the Minister reading the first verse, the people the second, and so on.

Who redeemeth thy life from destruction; who crowneth thee with loving-kindness and tender mercies.

The Lord is merciful and gracious; slow to anger, and plenteous in mercy.

He hath not dealt with us after our sins; nor rewarded us according to our iniquities.

For as the heaven is high above the earth; so great is His mercy toward them that fear Him.

As far as the East is from the West; so far hath He removed our transgressions from us.

Like as a father pitieth his children; so the Lord pitieth them that fear Him.

[Who hath not spared His Own Son, but delivered Him up for us all, and given us all things with Him. Therefore God commendeth therewith His love toward us, in that while we were yet sinners, Christ died for us; much more then, being now justified by His blood, we shall be saved from wrath through Him. For, if, when we were enemies, we were reconciled to God by the death of His Son; much more, being reconciled, we shall be saved by His life. Therefore shall my mouth and heart show forth the praise of the Lord from this time forth for evermore.] Amen.

**Let every one say with an attentive heart:**

O Almighty, Merciful God and Father, we render Thee most humble and hearty thanks, that Thou hast, of Thine infinite mercy, given us Thine Only Begotten Son, for a Mediator and a Sacrifice for our sins, and to be our Meat and Drink unto life eternal; and that Thou givest us lively faith, whereby we are made partakers of these Thy benefits.

Thou hast also been pleased, that Thy Beloved Son Jesus Christ should institute and ordain His Holy Supper for the confirmation of the same. Grant, we beseech Thee, O Faithful God and Father, that through the operation of Thy Holy Spirit, the commemoration of the death of our Lord Jesus Christ may tend to the daily increase of our faith, and of our saving fellowship with Him: Through Jesus Christ Thy Son, in whose Name we conclude our prayers, saying:

OUR FATHER WHO ART IN HEAVEN, HALLOWED BE THY NAME: THY KINGDOM COME: THY WILL BE DONE ON EARTH AS IT IS IN HEAVEN: GIVE US THIS DAY OUR DAILY BREAD: AND FORGIVE US OUR DEBTS, AS WE FORGIVE OUR DEBTORS: AND LEAD US NOT INTO TEMPTATION, BUT DELIVER US FROM EVIL: FOR THINE IS THE KINGDOM, AND THE POWER, AND THE GLORY, FOR EVER. AMEN.

# CHURCH DISCIPLINE.

## VI.

### Excommunication.

Beloved in the Lord Jesus Christ, it is known unto you, that we have several times, and by several methods declared unto you the great sin committed, and the heinous offence given by our fellow member N., to the end that he, by your Christian admonition, and prayers to God, might be brought to repentance, and so be freed from the bonds of the devil by whom he is held captive, and be recovered by the will of the Lord. But we cannot conceal from you, with great sorrow, that no one has as yet appeared before us, who hath in the least given us to understand that he, by the frequent admonitions given him, as well in private, as before witnesses, and in the presence of many, is come to any remorse for his sins, or hath shown the least token of true repentance. Since then by his stubbornness, he daily aggravates his sin, which in itself is not small, and since we lately signified unto you that in case he did not repent, after such patience shown him by the Church, we should be under the disagreeable necessity of being further grieved for him, and should come to the last remedy : we at this present are necessitated to proceed to this excommunication, according to the command and charge given us by God in his Holy Word; to the end that he may hereby be made, if possible, ashamed of his sins ; and likewise that we may not, by this rotten, and as yet incurable member, put the whole body of the Church in danger, and that God's Name may not be blasphemed.

Therefore, we, the Ministers and rulers of the Church of God, being here assembled ; in the name and authority of our Lord Jesus Christ, declare before you all, that for the aforesaid reasons we have excommunicated, and by these do excommunicate N. from the Church of God, and from the fellowship of Christ and of the Holy Sacraments, and from all the spiritual blessings and benefits, which God promises to and bestows upon His Church, so long as he obstinately and impenitently persists in his sins ; and he is therefore to be accounted by you as a heathen man and a publican, according to the command of Christ, who saith that whatsoever His ministers shall bind on earth, shall be bound in heaven.

Further, we exhort you, beloved Christians, to keep no company with him, that he may be ashamed ; yet count him not as an enemy, but at all times admonish him as you would a brother. In the mean time let every one take warning by this and such like examples, to fear the Lord, and diligently take heed unto himself, *if he thinketh he standeth, lest he fall;* but having true fellowship with the Father and His Son Jesus Christ, together with all faithful Christians, remain steadfast therein to the end, and so to obtain eternal salvation! You have seen, beloved brethren and sisters, in what manner this our excomunicated brother has begun to fall, and by degrees is come to ruin; observe, therefore, how subtle Satan is, to bring man to destruction, and to withdraw him from all salutary means of salvation. Guard, then, against the least beginnings of evil, " and laying aside every weight and the sin which doth so easily beset us, let us run with patience the race that is set before us, looking unto Jesus the Author and Finisher of our faith. Be sober; watch and pray, lest you enter into temptation. To-day, if you will hear the voice of the Lord, harden not your hearts, but work out your own salvation with fear and trembling;" and let every one repent of his sins, that our God may not humble us again, and we be obliged to bewail some one of you; but that you, living with one accord in all godliness, may be our crown and joy in the Lord.

Since it is God who worketh in us, both to will and to do of his good pleasure, let us call upon His Holy Name with confession of our sins, saying:

## PRAYER.

O Righteous God and Merciful Father, we bewail our sins before Thy High Majesty, and acknowledge that we have deserved the grief and sorrow caused us by the cutting off of this our late fellow member; yea, shouldst Thou enter into judgment with us, we all deserve, by reason of our great transgressions, to be cut off and banished from Thy presence. But, O Lord, Thou art merciful unto us for Christ's sake; forgive us our trespasses, for we heartily repent of them, and daily work in our hearts a greater measure of sorrow for them; that we, fearing Thy judgments which Thou executest against the stiff-necked, may endeavor to please Thee. Help us to avoid all pollution of the world, and of those who are cut off from the communion of the Church, that we may not make ourselves partakers of their sins; and grant that he, who is excommunicated, may become ashamed of his sins. And since Thou desirest not the death of a sinner. but that he may repent and live, and since the bosom of Thy Church is alway open for those, who turn away from their wickedness; we, therefore, humbly beseech Thee, to kindle in our hearts a pious zeal, that we may labor, with Christian admonitions and examples, to bring again this excommunicated person into the right way, together with all those who, through unbelief or dissoluteness of life, go astray.

Give Thy blessing to our admonitions, that we may have reason thereby to rejoice again in him, for whom we must now mourn; and that Thy Holy Name may be praised, through our Lord Jesus Christ, Who hath taught us to pray:

OUR FATHER WHO ART IN HEAVEN, HALLOWED BE THY NAME: THY KINGDOM COME: THY WILL BE DONE ON EARTH AS IT IS IN HEAVEN: GIVE US THIS DAY OUR DAILY BREAD: AND FORGIVE US OUR DEBTS, AS WE FORGIVE OUR DEBTORS: AND LEAD US NOT INTO TEMPTATION, BUT DELIVER US FROM EVIL: FOR THINE IS THE KINGDOM, AND THE POWER, AND THE GLORY, FOR EVER. AMEN.

II.

## Readmitting Excommunicated Persons
### INTO THE CHURCH OF CHRIST.

BELOVED IN THE LORD, it is known unto you, that some time ago our fellow member N. was cut off from the Church of Christ; we cannot now conceal from you, that he, by the above mentioned remedy, as also by the means of good admonition and your Christian prayers, is come so far, that he is ashamed of his sins, praying us to be re-admitted into the communion of the Church.

Since we then, by virtue of the command of God, are in duty bound to receive such persons with joy, and it being necessary that good order should be used therein, we therefore give you to understand hereby, that we purpose to loose again the aforementioned excommunicated person from the bond of excommunication, the next time when by the grace of God we celebrate the Supper of the Lord, and receive him again into the communion of the Church; except any one of you, in the mean time, shall show just cause why this ought not to be done, of which you must give notice to us in due time. In the mean time, let every one thank the Lord for the mercy shown this poor sinner, beseeching Him to perfect his work in him to his eternal salvation. AMEN.

<small>Afterwards, if no impediment be alleged, the Minister shall proceed to the re-admission of the excommunicated person, in the following manner:</small>

BELOVED CHRISTIANS, we have the last time informed you of the repentance of our fellow member N. to the end that he might with your foreknowledge be received into the Church of Christ; and whereas no one has alleged any thing why his re-admission ought not to take place, we therefore, at present, purpose to proceed to the same.

Our Lord Jesus Christ, Matt. 18, having confirmed the sentence of His Church, in the excommunication of impenitent sinners, declareth immediately thereupon, *that whatsoever his Ministers shall loose on earth, shall be loosed in heaven;* whereby He giveth to understand, that when any person is cut off from His Church he is not deprived of all hope of salvation; but can again be loosed from the bonds of condemnation. Therefore, since God declares in His Word, that He takes no pleasure in the death of a sinner, but that he turn from his wickedness and live, so the Church always hopes for the repentance of the backsliding sinner, and keepeth her bosom open to receive the penitent; accordingly the Apostle Paul, 1 Cor. 5, commanded the Corinthian (whom he had declared ought to be cut off from the Church) to be again received and comforted, since being reproved by many, he was come to the knowledge of his sins: to the end that he should not be swallowed up with over-much sorrow. 2 Cor. 2.

*Secondly*, Christ teaches us in the aforementioned text, that the sentence of absolution, which is passed upon such a penitent sinner according to the word of God, is counted sure and firm by the Lord; therefore, no one ought to doubt in the least, who truly repents, that he is assuredly received by God in mercy, as Christ saith, John, Chap. 20, *Whose soever sins ye remit, they are remitted unto them.*

But now to proceed to the matter in hand: I ask thee, N. whether thou dost declare here with all thine heart before God and His Church, that thou art sincerely sorry for the sin and stubbornness, for which thou hast justly been cut off from the Church: whether thou dost also truly believe, that the Lord hath forgiven thee, and doth forgive thy sins for Christ's sake, and that thou therefore art desirous to be re-admitted into the Church of Christ, promising henceforth to live in all godliness according to the command of the Lord?

*Answer.* Yes, verily.

Then the Minister shall further say,

We, then, here assembled in the Name and authority of the Lord Jesus Christ, declare thee N. to be absolved from the bonds of excommunication; and do receive thee again into the Church of the Lord, and declare unto thee that thou art in the communion of Christ and of the Holy Sacraments, and of all the spiritual blessings and benefits of God which He promiseth to and bestoweth upon His Church: may the Eternal God preserve thee therein, to the end, through His only begotten Son, Jesus Christ. AMEN.

Be therefore assured in thy heart, my beloved brother, that the Lord hath again received thee in mercy. Be diligent henceforward to guard thyself against the subtlety of Satan, and the wickedness of the world, to the end that thou mayest not fall again into sin: love Christ, for many sins are forgiven thee.

And you, beloved Christians, receive this your brother with hearty affection; be glad that he was dead and is alive again, he was lost and is found; rejoice with the angels of heaven, over this sinner who repenteth: count him no longer as a stranger, but as a fellow citizen with the saints, and of the household of God. And whereas we can have no good of ourselves, let us, praising and magnifying the Lord Almighty, implore His mercy, saying,

### PRAYER.

GRACIOUS GOD AND FATHER, we thank Thee, through Jesus Christ, that Thou hast been pleased to give this our fellow brother repentance unto life, and us cause to rejoice in his conversion. We beseech Thee, show him Thy mercy, that he may become more and more assured in his mind of the remission of his sins, and that he may receive from thence inexpressible joy and delight to serve Thee. And whereas he hath heretofore by his sins offended many, grant that he may, by his conversion, edify many. Grant also that he may steadfastly walk in Thy ways, to the end; and may we learn from this example, that with Thee is mercy, that Thou mayest be feared; and that we, counting him for our brother and co-heir of life eternal, may jointly serve Thee with filial fear and obedience all the days ot our life, through Jesus Christ our Lord, in whose Name we thus conclude our prayer:

OUR FATHER, WHO ART IN HEAVEN, HALLOWED BE THY NAME: THY KINGDOM COME: THY WILL BE DONE ON EARTH, AS IT IS IN HEAVEN: GIVE US THIS DAY OUR DAILY BREAD: AND FORGIVE US OUR DEBTS, AS WE FORGIVE OUR DEBTORS: AND LEAD US NOT INTO TEMPTATION, BUT DELIVER US FROM EVIL: FOR THINE IS THE KINGDOM, AND THE POWER, AND THE GLORY, FOR EVER. AMEN.

# FORMS OF ORDINATION.

## VII.

### I.

### For Ordaining the Ministers of God's Word.

*The sermon and the usual prayers being finished, the Minister shall thus speak to the Congregation:*

BELOVED BRETHREN: it is known unto you, that we have now at three different times published the name of our brother N., here present, to learn whether any person had aught to offer concerning his doctrine or life, why he might not be ordained to the Ministry of the Word. And, whereas, no one hath appeared before us, who hath alleged any thing lawful against his person, we shall therefore at present, in the Name of the Lord, proceed to his ordination. For which purpose, you N., and all those who are here present, shall first attend to a short declaration taken from the Word of God, touching the Institution and the Office of Pastors and Ministers of God's Word:

Where, in the first place, you are to observe, that God our Heavenly Father, willing to call and gather a Church from amongst the corrupt race of men unto life eternal, doth by a particular mark of His favor use the ministry of men therein. Therefore the Apostle Paul saith, that the Lord Jesus Christ "gave some, apostles; and some, prophets; and some, evangelists; and some, pastors and teachers; for the perfecting of the saints, for the work of the ministry, for the edifying of the body of Christ." Here we see that the Holy Apostle among other things saith, that the Pastoral office is an Institution of Christ.

What this Holy Office enjoins, may easily be gathered from the very name itself; for as it is the duty of a common shepherd, to feed, guide, protect, and rule the flock committed to his charge; so it is with regard to these spiritual shepherds, who are set over the Church which God calleth unto salvation, and counts as sheep of His pasture. The pasture with which these sheep are fed, is nothing but the preaching of the Gospel, accompanied with Prayer, and the administration of the Holy Sacraments. The same Word of God is likewise the staff with which the flock is guided and ruled. Consequently, it is evident that the office of Pastors and Ministers of God's Word is:

*First*, That they faithfully explain to their flock, the Word of the Lord, revealed by the writings of the prophets and the apostles; and apply the same, as well in general as in particular, to the edification of the hearers; instructing, admonishing, comforting, and reproving, according to every one's need; preaching repentance towards God, and reconciliation with Him through faith in Christ; and refuting with the Holy Scriptures all schisms and heresies which are repugnant to the pure doctrine. All this is clearly signified to us in Holy Writ; for the Apostle Paul saith, that these labor in the Word; and elsewhere he teaches that this must be done according to the measure [or rule] of faith. He writes also that a Pastor must hold fast and rightly divide the faithful and sincere Word which is according to the doctrine: "likewise, he that prophesieth [that is, preacheth God's Word], speaketh unto men to edification, and exhortation, and comfort." In another place, he proposes himself as a pattern to Pastors, declaring that he "publicly, and from house to house, taught, and testified repentance towards God, and faith towards our Lord Jesus Christ." But particularly we have a clear description of the office of Ministers of God's Word, (2 Cor. 5: 18–20), where the Apostle thus speaketh, "And all things are of God, who hath reconciled us to Himself by Jesus Christ, and hath given to us [namely to the Apostles and Pastors], the ministry of reconciliation; to wit, that God was in Christ, reconciling the world unto Himself, not imputing their trespasses unto them; and hath committed unto us the word of reconciliation. Now, then, we are ambassadors for Christ, as though God did beseech you by us: we pray you in Christ's stead, be ye reconciled to God." Concerning the refutation of false doctrine, the same Apostle saith (Tit. 1 : 9), that a Minister must "hold fast the faithful Word of God, that he may be able by sound doctrine both to exhort and convince the gainsayers."

*Secondly.* It is the Office of the Ministers, publicly to call upon the Name of the Lord in behalf of the whole congregation; for that which the Apostles say, "We will give ourselves continually to prayer, and to the ministry of the Word," is common to these Pastors and the Apostles; to which St. Paul, alluding, thus speaketh to Timothy: "I exhort, therefore, that, first of all, supplications, prayers, intercessions and giving of thanks, be made for all men: for kings, and for all that are in authority," etc., (1 Tim. 2: 1, 2).

*Thirdly.* Their Office is to administer the Sacraments which the Lord hath instituted as seals of His grace; as is evident from the command given by Christ to the Apostles, and in them to all Pastors: "Baptize them in the Name of the Father, and of the Son, and of the Holy Ghost." Likewise, "For I have received of the Lord that which also I delivered unto you," etc.

*Finally.* It is the duty of the Ministers of the Word, to keep the Church of God in good discipline, and to govern it in such a manner as the Lord hath ordained. For Christ, having spoken of the Christian discipline, says to His Apostles, "Whatsoever ye shall bind on earth shall be bound in heaven." And St. Paul will have the Ministers know how to rule their own house, since they otherwise neither can provide for, nor rule the Church of God. This is the reason why the Pastors are in Scripture called *Stewards of God and Bishops*, that is, overseers and watchmen; for they have the oversight of the house of God, wherein they are conversant, to the end that every thing may be transacted with good order and decency; and, also, that they may open and shut, with the keys of the Kingdom of Heaven committed to them, according to the charge given them by God.

From these things may be learned, what a glorious work the Ministerial Office is; since so great things are effected by it; yea, how highly necessary it is for man's salvation: which is also the reason why the Lord will have such an Office always to remain. For Christ said when He sent forth His Apostles to officiate in this holy function, "Lo, I am with you alway, even unto the end of the world;" where we see His pleasure is, that this Holy Office, (for the persons to whom he here speaketh could not live to the end of the world), should always be maintained on earth. And, therefore, St. Paul exhorted Timothy, "to commit that which he had heard of him to faithful men, who should be able to teach others"; as he also, having ordained Titus, minister, further commanded him to "ordain elders in every city," (Tit. 1 : 5).

Forasmuch therefore as we, for the maintaining of this office in the Church of God, are now to ordain a new Minister of the Word, and have sufficiently spoken of the Office of such persons; therefore you, N., shall answer to the following questions, to the end that it may appear to all here present, that you are inclined to accept of this Office as above described.

*First.* I ask thee, dost thou feel in thy heart that thou art lawfully called of God's Church, and, therefore, of God Himself, to this Holy Ministry?

*Secondly.* Dost thou believe the books of the Old

and New Testament to be the only Word of God, and the perfect doctrine unto salvation; and dost thou reject all doctrines repugnant thereto?

*Thirdly.* Dost thou promise faithfully to discharge thy office, according to the same doctrine as above described, and to adorn it with a godly life; also, to submit thyself, in case thou shouldst become delinquent, either in life or doctrine, to ecclesiastical admonition, according to the public ordinance of the churches?

To which the Candidate shall give answer.

*Answer.* Yes, truly, with all my heart.

Then the Minister, who did demand those questions of him, and other Ministers who are present, shall lay their hands * on his head, and say:

GOD, our Heavenly Father, who hath called thee to this Holy Ministry, enlighten thee with His Holy Spirit; strengthen thee with His hand; and so govern thee in thy Ministry, that thou mayest decently and fruitfully walk therein, to the glory of His Name, and the propagation of the Kingdom of His Son Jesus Christ. AMEN.

Then the Minister shall, from the pulpit, exhort the ordained Minister, and the congregation, in the following manner:

TAKE heed, therefore, beloved brother and fellow-servant in Christ, unto yourself and to all the flock, over which the Holy Ghost hath made you Overseer, to feed the Church of God which He hath purchased with His own blood: love Christ, and

---

* This ceremony shall not be used in ordaining those who have before been in the ministry.

feed His sheep, taking the oversight of them not by constraint, but willingly; not for filthy lucre, but of a ready mind; neither as being lord over God's heritage, but as an example to the flock. Be an example of believers, in word, in conversation, in charity, in spirit, in faith, in purity. Give attendance to reading, to exhortation, to doctrine. Neglect not the gift that is in thee; meditate upon these things; give thyself wholly to them, that thy profiting may appear to all; take heed to thy doctrine, and continue steadfast therein. Bear patiently all sufferings and oppressions, as a good soldier of Jesus Christ; for in doing this thou shalt both save thyself and them that hear thee. And when the Chief Shepherd shall appear, thou shalt receive a crown of glory that fadeth not away.

And you, likewise, beloved Christians, receive this your Minister in the Lord with all gladness, "and hold such in reputation." Remember that God Himself through him speaketh unto you and beseecheth you. Receive the word, which he, according to the Scripture, shall preach unto you, "not as the word of man, but, as it is in truth, the Word of God." Let the feet of those that preach the Gospel of Peace, and bring glad tidings of good things, be beautiful and pleasant unto you. Obey them that have the rule over you, and submit yourselves; for they watch for your souls, as they that must give account, that they may do it with joy, and not with grief; for that is unprofitable for you. If you do these things, it shall come to pass, that the peace of God shall enter into your houses, and that you, who receive this man in the name of a prophet, shall receive a prophet's reward, and through his preaching, believing in Christ, you shall through Christ inherit life eternal. Since no man is of himself fit for any of these things, let us call upon God with thanksgiving:

## PRAYER.

MERCIFUL FATHER, we thank Thee that it pleaseth Thee, by the ministry of men, to gather a Church to Thyself unto life eternal, from among the lost children of men. We bless Thee for so graciously providing the Church in this place with a faithful Minister. We beseech Thee to qualify him daily more and more by Thy Holy Spirit, for the ministry to which Thou hast ordained and called him. Enlighten his understanding to comprehend Thy Holy Word, and give him utterance, that he may boldly open his mouth, to make known and dispense the mysteries of the Gospel. Endue him with wisdom and valor to rule aright the people over which he is set, and to preserve them in Christian peace; to the end that Thy Church, under his administration and by his good example, may increase in number and in virtue. Grant him courage to bear the difficulties and troubles which he may meet with in his ministry; that being strengthened by the comfort of Thy Spirit, he may remain steadfast to the end, and be received with all faithful servants into the joy of His Master.

Give Thy grace also to this people and Church,

that they may becomingly deport themselves towards this their Minister; that they may acknowledge him to be sent of Thee; that they may receive his doctrine with all reverence and submit themselves to his exhortations; to the end that they may, by his word, believing in Christ, be made partakers of eternal life. Hear us, O Father, through Thy Beloved Son, who hath taught us to pray:

OUR FATHER WHO ART IN HEAVEN, HALLOWED BE THY NAME: THY KINGDOM COME: THY WILL BE DONE ON EARTH AS IT IS IN HEAVEN: GIVE US THIS DAY OUR DAILY BREAD: AND FORGIVE US OUR DEBTS, AS WE FORGIVE OUR DEBTORS: AND LEAD US NOT INTO TEMPTATION, BUT DELIVER US FROM EVIL: FOR THINE IS THE KINGDOM, AND THE POWER, AND THE GLORY, FOR EVER. AMEN.

## II.

### For Ordaining Elders and Deacons.

When Ordained at the same time ; if Ordained separately, this Form shall bo used as occasion requires.

BELOVED CHRISTIANS: you know that we have several times published unto you the names of our brethren here present, who are chosen to the office of Elders and Deacons in this Church, to the end that we might know whether any person had aught to allege, why they should not be ordained to their respective offices. And, whereas, no one hath appeared before us, who hath alleged any thing lawful against them, we shall, therefore, at present, in the name of the Lord, proceed to their ordination.

But first, you, who are to be ordained, and all those who are here present, shall attend to a short declaration [from the Word of God,] concerning [the institution and] the office of Elders and Deacons.

[Of the ELDERS it is to be observed, that the word Elder or Eldest (which is taken out of the Old Testament, and signifieth a person who is placed in an honorable office of government over others) is applied to two sorts of persons who administer in the Church of Jesus Christ: for the Apostle saith, "the Elders that rule well shall be counted worthy of double honor, especially they who labor in the Word and doctrine." Hence, it is evident that there were two sorts of Elders in the Apostolic Church, the former whereof did labor in the Word and doctrine, and the latter did not. The first were the Ministers of the Word and Pastors, who preached the Gospel and administered the Sacraments ; but the others, who did not labor in the Word, and still did serve in the Church, bore a particular office, namely, that they had the oversight of the Church, and ruled the same with the Ministers of the Word. For St. Paul (Rom. 12:8), having spoken of the ministry of the Word, and also of the office of distribution of deaconship speaketh afterwards particularly of this office, saying: "He that ruleth, let him do it with diligence;" likewise, in another place, he counts "governments" among the gifts and offices which God hath instituted in the Church (1 Cor. 12:28). Thus we see that these sorts of Ministers are added to the others who preach the Gospel, to aid and assist them, as in the Old Testament the common Levites were to the priests in the service of the tabernacle, in those things which they could not perform alone; notwithstanding, the offices always remained distinct one from the other.

Moreover, it is proper that such men should be joined to the Ministers of the Word in the government of the Church, that thereby all tyranny and lording may be kept out of the Church of God which may sooner creep in, when the government is placed in the hands of one alone, or of a very few. And thus, the Ministers of the Word, together with the Elders, form a body or assembly, being as a council of the Church, representing the whole Church; to which Christ alludes when He saith: "Tell the Church;" which can in no wise be understood of all and every member of the Church, in particular, but very properly of those who govern the Church out of which they are chosen.

Therefore,] In the *first* place, the office of the Elders is, together with the Ministers of the Word, to take the oversight of the Church, which is committed to them, and diligently to look, whether every one properly deports himself in his confession and conversation; to admonish those who behave themselves disorderly, and to prevent, as much as possible, the Sacraments from being profaned; also to act, according to the Christian discipline, against the impenitent, and to receive the penitent again into the bosom of the Church: as it doth appear, not only from the above-mentioned saying of Christ, but also from many other places of Holy Writ (as 1 Cor. 5, and 2 Cor. 2), that these things are not entrusted to only one or two persons, but to many who are ordained thereto.

*Secondly.* Since the Apostle enjoineth, that all things shall be done decently and in order, amongst Christians, and that no other persons ought to serve in the Church of Christ but those who are lawfully called, according to the Christian ordinance; therefore it is also the duty of the Elders to pay regard to it, and in all occurrences which relate to the welfare and good order of the Church, to be assistant with their good counsel and advice to the Ministers of the Word; yea, also, to serve all Christians with advice and consolation.

*Thirdly.* It is also their duty particularly to have regard unto the doctrine and conversation of the Ministers of the Word, to the end that all things may be directed to the edification of the Church; and that no strange doctrine be taught, according to that which we read (Acts 20), where the Apostle exhorteth to watch diligently against the wolves, which might come into the sheep-fold of Christ: for the performance of which the Elders are in duty bound diligently to search the Word of God:

[and continually to be meditating on the mysteries of faith.]

Concerning the DEACONS: of the origin and institution of their office we may read, Acts 6, where we find that the Apostles themselves did in the beginning serve the poor, " At whose feet was brought the price of the things that were sold: and distribution was made unto every man according as he had need. But afterwards, when a murmuring arose, because the widows of the Grecians were neglected in the daily ministration," men were chosen, by the advice of the Apostles, who should make the service of the poor their peculiar business, to the end that the Apostles might continually give themselves to prayer, and to the Ministry of the Word.

[And this has been continued from that time forward in the Church, as appears from Rom. 12:8, where the Apostle, speaking of this office, saith, "he that giveth, let him do it with simplicity." And (1 Cor. 12:28), speaking of "helps," he means those who are appointed in the Church to help and assist the poor and indigent in time of need]; from which [passage] we may easily gather, what the Deacons office is; namely:

That they, in the *first* place, collect and preserve, with greatest fidelity and diligence, the alms and goods which are given to the poor; yea, use their utmost endeavors, that many good means be procured for the relief of the poor.

The *second* part of their office consists in distribution; wherein are required not only discretion and prudence, to bestow the alms [only on the objects of charity,] but also cheerfulness and simplicity to assist the poor with compassion and hearty affection; as the Apostle requires, (Rom 12, and 2 Cor. 9). For which end it is very beneficial, that they administer relief to the poor and indigent, not only with external gifts, but also with comfortable words from Scripture.

To the end, therefore, beloved brethren, N., N., that every one may hear that you are willing to take your respective offices upon you, ye shall answer the following questions:

And, in the *first* place, I ask you, both Elders and Deacons, whether ye feel in your hearts, that ye are lawfully called of God's Church, and consequently of God Himself, to these your respective holy offices?

*Secondly.* Do ye believe the books of the Old and New Testament to be the only Word of God, and the perfect doctrine of salvation; and do ye reject all doctrines repugnant thereto?

*Thirdly.* Do ye promise, agreeably to said doctrine, faithfully according to your ability, to discharge your respective offices, as they are here described: Ye Elders, in the government of the Church together with the Ministers of the Word: and ye Deacons, in the ministrations to the poor: Do ye also jointly promise to walk in all godliness, and to submit yourselves, in case ye should become remiss in your duty, to the admonitions of the Church?

Upon which they shall answer:

Yes.

Then the Minister shall say:

The Almighty God and Father replenish you all with His grace, that ye may faithfully and fruitfully discharge your respective offices. AMEN.

*The Minister shall further exhort them, and the whole congregation, in the following manner:*

Therefore, ye Elders, be diligent in the government of the Church, which is committed to you and the Ministers of the Word. Be ye also, as watchmen over the house and city of God, faithful to admonish and to caution every one against his ruin. Take heed that purity of doctrine and godliness of life be maintained in the Church of God. And, ye Deacons, be diligent in collecting the alms, prudent and cheerful in the distribution of the same: assist the oppressed, provide for the true widows and orphans, show liberality unto all men, but especially to the household of faith. Be ye all with one accord faithful in your offices, and hold the mystery of the faith in a pure conscience, being good examples unto all the people. In so doing you will purchase to yourselves a good degree, and great boldness in the faith which is in Christ Jesus; and hereafter enter into the joy of your Lord.

On the other hand, beloved Christians, receive these men as the servants of God. Count the Elders that rule well, worthy of double honor, give yourselves willingly to their inspection and government. Provide the Deacons with good means to assist the indigent. Be charitable, [ye rich]; give liberally, and contribute willingly.

[And, ye poor, be poor in spirit, and deport yourself respectfully towards your benefactors, be thankful to them, and avoid murmuring; follow Christ, for the food of your souls, but not for bread. Let him that stole [or hath been burthensome to his neighbor] steal no more; but rather let him labor, working with his hands the thing which is good, that he may have to give to him that needeth."

Each of you, doing these things in your respective callings, shall receive of the Lord, the reward of righteousness. But since we are unable of ourselves, let us call upon the name of the Lord, saying:

## PRAYER.

O LORD GOD and Heavenly Father, we thank Thee that it hath pleased Thee, for the better edification of Thy Church, to ordain in it besides the Ministers of the Word, rulers and assistants, by whom Thy Church may be preserved in peace and prosperity, and the indigent assisted; and that Thou hast at present granted us in this place men who are of good testimony, and we hope endowed with Thy Spirit. We beseech Thee, replenish them more and more with such gifts as may be necessary for them in their ministrations; with the gifts of wisdom, courage, discretion, and benevolence; to the end that every one, may, in his respective office, acquit himself as is becoming; the Elders, in taking diligent heed unto the doctrine and conversation, in keeping out the wolves from the sheepfold of Thy beloved Son, and in admonishing and reproving disorderly persons: in like manner the Deacons, in carefully receiving, and liberally and prudently distributing the alms [to the poor,] and in comforting [them] with Thy Holy Word. Give grace both to the Elders and Deacons, that they may persevere in their faithful labor, and never become weary by reason of any trouble, pain or persecution of the world. Grant, also, especially Thy divine grace to this people, over whom they are placed, that they may willingly submit themselves to the good exhortations of the Elders, counting them worthy of honor for their works' sake; give also unto the rich liberal hearts towards the poor, and to the poor, grateful hearts towards those who help and serve them; to the end that every one acquitting himself of his duty, Thy Holy Name may thereby be magnified, and the kingdom of Thy Son Jesus Christ, enlarged, in whose Name we conclude our prayers:

OUR FATHER WHO ART IN HEAVEN, HALLOWED BE THY NAME: THY KINGDOM COME: THY WILL BE DONE ON EARTH AS IT IS IN HEAVEN: GIVE US THIS DAY OUR DAILY BREAD: AND FORGIVE US OUR DEBTS, AS WE FORGIVE OUR DEBTORS: AND LEAD US NOT INTO TEMPTATION, BUT DELIVER US FROM EVIL: FOR THINE IS THE KINGDOM, AND THE POWER, AND THE GLORY, FOR EVER. AMEN.

# VIII.

## Office for the Installation of a Minister.

*The sermon and usual prayers being ended, the Minister presiding shall say:*

BELOVED BRETHREN: it is known unto you that at three separate times, has been published to you the name of our brother, here present, to learn whether any person had aught to allege concerning his doctrine or life, why he might not be installed Minister of this church: And whereas no lawful objection has been presented, we shall, therefore, in the Name of the Lord, proceed to his installation.

For His own glory in the salvation of men, it hath pleased our Lord Jesus Christ to institute various offices in His Church. Accordingly, it is declared in Holy Scripture, that our ascended Lord hath given "some, apostles, and some, prophets, and some, evangelists, and some, pastors and teachers, for the perfecting of the saints, for the work of the ministry, for the edifying of the body of Christ." Of these, in the present condition of the Church, the pastoral office is the first both in dignity and responsibility. It is instituted by our Lord Jesus Christ.

It belongs to the Office of a Minister of Christ to present the worship of the people to God; to read the Holy Scriptures in the public service; to feed the flock committed to his charge with the pure Gospel of Christ; to administer the Holy Sacraments agreeably to the institution of Christ; to maintain Christian discipline; to comfort them that are afflicted in mind, body, or estate; to reclaim the erring, having compassion on the ignorant, and on them that are out of the way; to teach, direct, counsel as a father, the children; and thus, in all vigilant and faithful service to make full proof of his ministry.

In the discharge of these holy functions, he is entitled to the respect, gratitude, love, and obedience of the people of his charge. It is incumbent on them by the will and command of Him that sent him, to receive him as the ambassador of Christ. By a suitable maintenance to enable him to provide things honest in the sight of all men; to keep him free of distracting care; to guard jealously his reputation; to wait on his ministry with reverence and affection; to help him by generous sympathy, and faithful fellow-working and earnest prayer; to submit to his guidance; to further his work, and to be followers of him as he is of Christ; as the holy Apostle enjoins:

"Obey them that have the rule over you, and submit yourselves, for they watch for your souls as they that must give account, that they may do it with joy and not with grief;" and again, "We beseech you to know them which labor among you, and are over you in the Lord, and to esteem them very highly in love for their work's sake."

To the end, then, beloved Brother and fellow-Minister of Christ, that it may appear that thou art willing to take the oversight of this flock of God, to which He has called thee in His holy providence, we demand of thee, in the presence of God and these witnesses:

1. Dost thou believe the books of the Old and New Testament to be the only Word of God and the perfect doctrine unto salvation, and dost thou reject all doctrines repugnant thereto?

2. Dost thou promise faithfully to discharge thine office according to the same doctrine, and to adorn it with a godly life; also to submit thyself, in case thou shouldst become delinquent either in life or doctrine, to ecclesiastical admonition, according to the public ordinance of the churches?

3. Wilt thou with the help of God, fulfil all the duty of a faithful Minister of Christ to this Church, preaching the Word of God in sincerity, administering the Holy Sacraments in purity; maintaining proper discipline in the house of God; and using thy whole endeavor to promote the denominational work and welfare of the Reformed Church in America?

To which the Minister Elect shall give answer:

Yes, truly, with all my heart.

*Then the Minister presiding shall say :*

God, our Heavenly Father, who hath called thee to the Holy Ministry, and to take the oversight of this Church, enlighten thee with His Holy Spirit; strengthen thee with His hand ; and so govern thee in thy Ministry, that thou mayest decently and fruitfully walk therein, to the glory of His Name, and to the advancement of the Kingdom of His Son Jesus Christ. AMEN.

*The Church having been requested to arise, the Minister Presiding shall say :*

Inasmuch, Beloved Brethren and Members of this Church, as this most solemn procedure of investing our brother with the charge and oversight of you, involves, as well, obligations and duties on your part toward him : I ask of you before God and our Lord Jesus Christ :

1. Do you hereby receive, in the Name of the Lord, His servant, our brother, to be your Minister ?

2. Do you promise to receive the word of truth from his lips with meekness and love ; and to submit to him in the due discharge of his Holy Office ?

3. Do you promise to give him all proper love and obedience in the Lord ; to encourage and help him in his holy work; and to labor with him in faith and prayer, for the honor of Christ and the welfare of men ?

4. Do you engage to continue to him, while he remains your Minister, competent worldly maintenance, as you have promised, and whatever else

the honor of religion and his comfort among you may require?

To which they shall give answer audibly:
YES!

Then the Minister Presiding shall exhort the installed Minister and Congregation in the following manner:

TAKE heed, therefore, beloved brother, and fellow-servant in Christ, unto yourself and to all the flock, over which the Holy Ghost hath made you Overseer, to feed the Church of God which He hath purchased with His own blood: love Christ, and feed His sheep, taking the oversight of them not by constraint, but willingly: not for filthy lucre, but of a ready mind; neither as being lord over God's heritage, but as an example to the flock. Be an example of believers, in word, in conversation, in charity, in spirit, in faith, in purity. Give attendance to reading, to exhortation, to doctrine. Neglect not the gift that is in thee; meditate upon these things, give thyself wholly to them, that thy profiting may appear to all: take heed to thy doctrine, and continue steadfast therein. Bear patiently all hardship, as a good soldier of Jesus Christ, for in doing this thou shalt both save thyself and them that hear thee. And when the Chief Shepherd shall appear, thou shalt receive a crown of glory that fadeth not away.

And you likewise, beloved Christians, receive this your Minister in the Lord, with all gladness, "and hold such in reputation." Remember that God Himself, through him, speaketh unto you and beseecheth you. Receive the Word, which he, according to the Scripture, shall preach unto you, "not as the word of man, but (as it is in truth) the Word of God." Let the feet of those that preach the Gospel of peace, and bring glad tidings of good things, be beautiful and pleasant unto you. Obey them that have the rule over you, and submit yourselves; for they watch for your souls, as they that must give account, that they may do it with joy and not with grief; for that is unprofitable for you. If you do these things, it shall come to pass, that the peace of God shall enter into your houses, and that you who receive this man in the name of a prophet, shall receive a prophet's reward, and through his preaching, believing in Christ, you shall through Christ inherit life eternal.

Since no man is of himself fit for any of these things, let us call upon God with thanksgiving:

## PRAYER.

MERCIFUL FATHER, we thank Thee that it pleaseth Thee, by the ministry of men, to gather a Church to Thyself unto life eternal, from amongst the lost children of men. We bless Thee for so graciously providing the Church in this place with a faithful Minister. We beseech Thee to qualify him daily more and more by the Holy Spirit, for the ministry to which Thou hast ordained and called him. Enlighten his understanding to comprehend Thy Holy Word, and give him utterance, that he may boldly open his mouth, to make known and dispense the mysteries of the gospel. Endue him with wisdom and valor, to rule the people aright over whom he is set, and to preserve them in Christian peace; to the end that Thy Church, under his administration and by his good example, may increase in number and in virtue. Grant him courage to bear the difficulties and troubles which he may meet with in his ministry, that being strengthened by the comfort of Thy Spirit, he may remain steadfast to the end, and be received with all faithful servants into the joy of his Master.

Give Thy grace also to this people and Church, that they may becomingly deport themselves towards this their Minister; that they may acknowledge him to be sent of Thee; that they may receive his doctrine with all reverence, and submit themselves to his exhortations: to the end that they may by his word, believing in Christ, be made partakers of eternal life. Hear us, O Father, through Thy Beloved Son, who hath thus taught us to pray;

OUR FATHER WHO ART IN HEAVEN, HALLOWED BE THY NAME: THY KINGDOM COME: THY WILL BE DONE ON EARTH AS IT IS IN HEAVEN: GIVE US THIS DAY OUR DAILY BREAD: AND FORGIVE US OUR DEBTS, AS WE FORGIVE OUR DEBTORS: AND LEAD US NOT INTO TEMPTATION, BUT DELIVER US FROM EVIL: FOR THINE IS THE KINGDOM, AND THE POWER, AND THE GLORY, FOR EVER. AMEN.

# IX.

## Office for the Laying of the Corner-Stone of a Church or Chapel.

*The Minister officiating will begin the service with the Salutation:*

Grace be unto you and peace from God our Father, and from the Lord Jesus Christ. AMEN.

*After which he will say:*

DEARLY BELOVED: We are here assembled in the name of the Triune God, Father, Son, and Holy Ghost, to lay the corner-stone of a house to be erected to His honor and service, and praise. Within its walls His Holy Name is to be worshipped, His Holy Gospel is to be preached, and His Holy Sacraments administered. Knowing that our help is the name of the Lord Who made heaven and earth, let us lift up our hearts unto Him in humble supplication for His blessing.

### PRAYER.

O Almighty God, Who hast built Thy Church upon the foundation of the Apostles and Prophets,

Jesus Christ Himself being the Chief Cornerstone; direct us in this our undertaking with Thy most gracious favor, and further us with Thy continual help, that all our work being begun, continued, and ended in Thee, we may glorify Thy Holy Name; and finally, by Thy mercy, obtain everlasting life through Jesus Christ our Lord. AMEN.

Then shall be chanted or read responsively from the Scriptures of the Old Testament:

## PSALM 87.

1. HIS foundation *is* in the holy mountains.
2. THE LORD LOVETH THE GATES OF ZION MORE THAN ALL THE DWELLINGS OF JACOB.
3. Glorious things are spoken of thee, O city of God.
4. I WILL MAKE MENTION OF RAHAB AND BABYLON TO THEM THAT KNOW ME: BEHOLD PHILISTIA AND TYRE, WITH ETHIOPIA: THIS MAN WAS BORN THERE.
5. And of Zion it shall be said, This and that man was born in her: and the Highest Himself shall establish her.
6. THE LORD SHALL COUNT, WHEN HE WRITETH UP THE PEOPLE THAT THIS MAN WAS BORN THERE.
7. As well the singers as the players on instruments *shall be there:* all my springs *are* in Thee.

And from the Scriptures of the New Testament, shall be read:

### 1 EP. OF ST. PETER 2: 1-9.

1. WHEREFORE, laying aside all malice, and all

guile, and hypocrisies, and envies, and all evil-speakings,

2. As new-born babes, desire the sincere milk of the word, that ye may grow thereby:

3. If so be ye have tasted that the Lord *is* gracious:

4. To Whom coming, *as unto* a Living Stone, disallowed indeed of men, but chosen of God, *and* precious:

5. Ye also, as lively stones, are built up a spiritual house, an holy priesthood, to offer up spiritual sacrifices, acceptable to God by Jesus Christ.

6. Wherefore also, it is contained in the scripture: Behold, I lay in Sion a Chief Corner-stone, elect, precious: and he that believeth on Him shall not be confounded.

7. Unto you therefore which believe, *He is* precious: but unto them which be disobedient, the stone which the builders disallowed, the same is made the Head of the corner,

8. And a stone of stumbling, and a rock of offence, *even to them* which stumble at the word, being disobedient; whereunto also they were appointed.

9. But ye *are* a chosen generation, a royal priesthood, an holy nation, a peculiar people; that ye should shew forth the praises of Him who hath called you out of darkness into His marvelous light.

Then, any such historical or descriptive document as may have been prepared to be deposited in the Corner-stone may be read, and the stone having been set in its place, the Minister, laying his hand upon it, or striking it thrice with a mallet, shall say:

I lay the Corner-stone of a house to be erected, and devoted to the service of Almighty God; in the Name of the Father, and of the Son, and of the Holy Ghost. AMEN.

Other foundation can no man lay than that is laid which is Jesus Christ.

Except the Lord build the house, they labor in vain that build it.

Then shall be repeated, in unison, the Apostle's Creed.

I BELIEVE IN GOD THE FATHER ALMIGHTY, MAKER OF HEAVEN AND EARTH;

AND IN JESUS CHRIST HIS ONLY SON OUR LORD; WHO WAS CONCEIVED BY THE HOLY GHOST; BORN OF THE VIRGIN MARY; SUFFERED UNDER PONTIUS PILATE; WAS CRUCIFIED, DEAD AND BURIED; HE DESCENDED INTO HELL; THE THIRD DAY HE ROSE AGAIN FROM THE DEAD; HE ASCENDED INTO HEAVEN; AND SITTETH AT THE RIGHT HAND OF GOD THE FATHER ALMIGHTY; FROM THENCE HE SHALL COME TO JUDGE THE QUICK AND THE DEAD.

I BELIEVE IN THE HOLY GHOST; THE HOLY CATHOLIC CHURCH, THE COMMUNION OF SAINTS; THE FORGIVENESS OF SINS; THE RESURRECTION OF THE BODY; AND THE LIFE EVERLASTING. AMEN.

After which may be sung a hymn. Then may follow an

## ADDRESS.

After which shall be offered the concluding prayer:

BLESSED be Thy Name, O Lord, that it hath pleased Thee to put it into the hearts of Thy servants to commence the erection of a house, in which Thy Name is to be worshipped, the Glad Tidings of salvation proclaimed, and Thy Holy Sacraments administered. Prosper them, O Lord, in this their undertaking. Keep and preserve by Thy providence unto the end, the work, which is now begun in Thy fear. Excite the skill and animate the industry of the workmen. Shield them from accident and danger. And grant unto them, and unto all of us here present, the influences of Thy Divine Spirit, so that we may become in soul and body, living temples of the Holy Ghost, and be prepared for that eternal city which hath foundations, whose Builder and Maker is God. All which we ask through the abundant merits of our Lord and Saviour Jesus Christ, Who liveth and reigneth with Thee and the Holy Ghost, ever One God, world without end.

OUR FATHER WHO ART IN HEAVEN, HALLOWED BE THY NAME: THY KINGDOM COME: THY WILL BE DONE ON EARTH AS IT IS IN HEAVEN: GIVE US THIS DAY OUR DAILY BREAD: AND FORGIVE US OUR DEBTS, AS WE FORGIVE OUR DEBTORS: AND LEAD US NOT INTO TEMPTATION, BUT DELIVER US FROM EVIL: FOR THINE IS THE KINGDOM, AND THE POWER, AND THE GLORY, FOR EVER. AMEN.

## BENEDICTION.

X.

# Office for the Dedication of a House of Worship.

The usual Order of Service for the Lord's Day having been observed until after the reading of the Commandments, the following Lessons from Holy Scripture shall then be read:

### 1.—From the Psalter

The Minister and People reading responsively.

## Psalm XXIV.

The earth *is* the LORD'S, and the fulness thereof; the world, and they that dwell therein.

FOR HE HATH FOUNDED IT UPON THE SEAS, AND ESTABLISHED IT UPON THE FLOODS.

Who shall ascend into the hill of the LORD? or who shall stand in His holy place?

HE THAT HATH CLEAN HANDS, AND A PURE HEART; WHO HATH NOT LIFTED UP HIS SOUL UNTO VANITY, NOR SWORN DECEITFULLY.

He shall receive the blessing from the LORD, and righteousness from the God of his salvation.

THIS IS THE GENERATION OF THEM THAT SEEK HIM, THAT SEEK THY FACE, O JACOB, SELAH,

Lift up your heads, O ye gates; and be ye lifted up, ye everlasting doors; and the King of glory shall come in.

WHO IS THIS KING OF GLORY? THE LORD STRONG AND MIGHTY, THE LORD MIGHTY IN BATTLE.

Lift up your heads, O ye gates; even lift *them* up, ye everlasting doors; and the King of glory shall come in.

WHO IS THIS KING OF GLORY? THE LORD OF HOSTS, HE IS THE KING OF GLORY.

## Psalm CXXXII.

1. LORD, remember David, *and* all his afflictions:
2. HOW HE SWARE UNTO THE LORD, AND VOWED UNTO THE MIGHTY GOD OF JACOB;
3. Surely I will not come into the tabernacle of my house, nor go up into my bed;
4. I WILL NOT GIVE SLEEP TO MINE EYES, OR SLUMBER TO MINE EYELIDS,
5. Until I find out a place for the LORD, a habitation for the mighty *God* of Jacob.
6. LO, WE HEARD OF IT AT EPHRATAH: WE FOUND IT IN THE FIELDS OF THE WOOD.
7. We will go into His tabernacles; we will worship at His footstool.
8. ARISE, O LORD, INTO THY REST: THOU, AND THE ARK OF THY STRENGTH.
9. Let Thy priests be clothed with righteousness; and let Thy saints shout for joy.
10. FOR THY SERVANT DAVID'S SAKE TURN NOT AWAY THE FACE OF THINE ANOINTED.
11. The LORD hath sworn in truth unto David; He will not turn from it; Of the fruit of thy body will I set upon thy throne.
12. IF THY CHILDREN WILL KEEP MY COVENANT AND MY TESTIMONY THAT I SHALL TEACH THEM, THEIR CHILDREN SHALL ALSO SIT UPON THY THRONE FOR EVERMORE.
13. For the Lord hath chosen Zion; He hath desired *it* for His habitation.
14. THIS IS MY REST FOR EVER: HERE WILL I DWELL FOR I HAVE DESIRED IT.
15. I will abundantly bless her provision; I will satisfy her poor with bread.
16. I WILL ALSO CLOTHE HER PRIESTS WITH SALVATION: AND HER SAINTS SHALL SHOUT ALOUD FOR JOY.
17. There will I make the horn of David to bud: I have ordained a lamp for Mine anointed.
18. HIS ENEMIES WILL I CLOTHE WITH SHAME: BUT UPON HIMSELF SHALL HIS CROWN FLOURISH.

## II.—From the Old Testament:

Exod. 40 : 17–38 ; or, 1 Kings, 9 : 1–9.

## III.—From the New Testament:

Heb. 13 : 10–21 ; or, Rev. 21 : 10–27.

**Then the Minister shall say :**

DEARLY BELOVED IN THE LORD: God our Heavenly Father, having in His grace, which is in Jesus Christ our Lord, brought to its consummation our work of preparing a house for His worship, and the honor of His Holy Name; within whose walls His Holy Gospel is to be truly preached and His Holy Sacraments are to be faithfully administered; we are now gathered in His Holy presence for the purpose of devoting it by a solemn act of worship to its proper and sacred use. I call upon you, therefore, to arise, and before the Lord, to unite in this act of dedication, confessing first, devoutly, our holy faith.

**The people uniting audibly with the Minister.**

I BELIEVE IN GOD THE FATHER ALMIGHTY, MAKER OF HEAVEN AND EARTH; AND IN JESUS CHRIST, HIS ONLY SON, OUR LORD; WHO WAS CONCEIVED BY THE HOLY GHOST; BORN OF THE VIRGIN MARY; SUFFERED UNDER PONTIUS PILATE; WAS CRUCIFIED, DEAD AND BURIED; HE DESCENDED INTO HELL; THE THIRD DAY HE ROSE AGAIN FROM THE DEAD; HE AS-

CENDED INTO HEAVEN, AND SITTETH AT THE RIGHT HAND OF GOD THE FATHER ALMIGHTY: FROM THENCE HE SHALL COME TO JUDGE THE QUICK AND THE DEAD.

I BELIEVE IN THE HOLY GHOST; THE HOLY CATHOLIC CHURCH, THE COMMUNION OF SAINTS; THE FORGIVENESS OF SINS; THE RESURRECTION OF THE BODY; AND THE LIFE EVERLASTING. AMEN.

*Then the Minister shall offer the*

## PRAYER OF DEDICATION.

*The People uniting audibly in the responses, which are printed in small capitals.*

HOLY, HOLY, HOLY, LORD GOD ALMIGHTY, Who art, and wast, and art to come, the whole earth is full of Thy glory! Thine, O Lord, is the greatness, and the power, and the glory, and the victory, and the majesty; for all that is in the heaven and in the earth is Thine: Now, therefore, we thank Thee, O God, and praise Thy glorious Name.

But who are we, that we should be able to offer so willingly after this sort? For all things come of Thee, and of Thine own do we give Thee. O Lord our God, all this store that we have prepared to build Thee an house for Thine Holy Name, cometh of Thine hand and is all Thine own.

Now behold, O Lord our God, and look unto this place where we are gathered in Thy Name; and have respect to the prayer of Thy servants and to their supplication, to hearken unto the cry and the prayer that Thy servants pray before Thee this day, to take this house for Thine Own.

Holy, Blessed, and Glorious Trinity, Three Persons in One God,
To THEE WE DEDICATE IT.

Father of our Lord Jesus Christ, Our Father Who art in Heaven,
To THEE WE DEDICATE IT.

Son of God, the Only Begotten of the Father, Head of the Body, which is the Church; Head over all things to the Church; Prophet, Priest and King of Thy people,
To THEE WE DEDICATE IT.

God the Holy Ghost, proceeding from the Father and the Son; given to be our abiding Teacher, Sanctifier, and Comforter; Lord and Giver of Life,
To THEE WE DEDICATE IT.

Arise, O Lord, into Thy rest, Thou and the ark of Thy strength. Let Thy priests be clothed with righteousness, and let Thy people shout for joy. Put Thy Name in this place. Sanctify it by Thy presence and Thy constant abiding. Give power and efficacy to Thy Gospel preached in it, and Thy Sacraments administered in it. Let Thine eyes be opened towards it; and hearken unto the supplications of Thy people when they pray in this place, and hear Thou in Heaven Thy dwelling-place, and when Thou hearest, forgive. And from this outer court of Thy Holy Sanctuary bring Thy people and their children into the true tabernacle which the Lord pitched, and not man; the heavenly temple, of which the Lord God Almighty and the Lamb are the light. We ask and offer all in the

Name of Thy Son our Saviour, Who hath taught us to pray:

OUR FATHER, WHO ART IN HEAVEN, HALLOWED BE THY NAME: THY KINGDOM COME: THY WILL BE DONE ON EARTH, AS IT IS IN HEAVEN: GIVE US THIS DAY OUR DAILY BREAD: AND FORGIVE US OUR DEBTS, AS WE FORGIVE OUR DEBTORS; AND LEAD US NOT INTO TEMPTATION, BUT DELIVER US FROM EVIL: FOR THINE IS THE KINGDOM, AND THE POWER, AND THE GLORY, FOR EVER. AMEN.

*Then shall follow the usual Order of Service, beginning with the Hymn before the Sermon.*

# XI.

## Office for the Confirmation of Marriage.

---

Our help is in the Name of the Lord Who made heaven and earth.

*The Minister shall say to all present:*

DEARLY BELOVED,
We are assembled, in the sight of God, to join together this man and this woman in the bonds of Marriage : which is an honorable estate, instituted of God in the time of man's innocency, confirmed by the teaching of our Blessed Saviour, and compared by St. Paul to the mystical union which subsists between Christ and His Church.

Into this holy estate these two persons are come to be joined. Therefore, if any man can show any just cause why they may not lawfully be joined together, let him now declare it, or else, hereafter, for ever hold his peace.

*And to those who come to be married :*

I charge you, each and both, as ye shall answer to Him Who will judge both quick and dead, if either of you know any reason why ye may not lawfully be joined together in marriage, declare it now. For, be well-assured that all those who are brought together contrary to the Word of God are not joined together of God, neither is their marriage lawful.

*If no sufficient impediment be alleged, the Minister shall say:*

Hear now what Holy Scripture doth teach, as touching the duty of husbands to their wives, and of wives to their husbands:

Husbands love your wives, even as Christ also loved the Church, and gave Himself for it, that He might sanctify and cleanse it with the washing of water by the Word. So ought men to love their wives as their own bodies. He that loveth his wife loveth himself. For this cause shall a man leave his father and mother and shall be joined unto his wife, and they two shall be one flesh. And,

Wives, submit yourselves unto your own husbands as unto the Lord. For the husband is the head of the wife, even as Christ is the Head of the Church. And He is the Saviour of the body. And again He saith, Let the wife see that she reverence her husband.

LET US PRAY.

O Most Holy and Most Merciful Lord God! we beseech Thee for these, Thy servant and handmaid, that they may, with a reverent trust in Thee, enter into the Covenant of Marriage, as they now propose, and truly keep all the vows which they are about to make, according to Thy Word. Grant this, O Father, with the forgiveness of our sins, through Christ Thy Son. AMEN.

*Then the Minister shall bid the man and the woman join their right hands; which being done, he shall say to the man:*

Dost thou, ———, take this woman,——— before God and these witnesses, to be thy wedded wife?

*The man shall answer,* I DO.

Wilt thou love her, comfort her, honor and keep her in sickness and in health, and forsaking every other, cleave to her only, so long as ye both shall live?

*The man shall answer,* I WILL.

*To the woman:*

Dost thou, ———, take this man,———, before God and these witnesses to be thy wedded husband?

*The woman shall answer,* I DO.

Wilt thou love, honor, reverence, and keep him, in sickness and in health, and forsaking every other, cleave to him only, so long as ye both shall live?

*The woman shall answer,* I WILL.

*Then when a ring is used, the Minister shall guide the hand of the man to put the ring on the third finger of the woman's left hand, and holding it there, the man shall say, after the Minister:*

With this ring I thee wed; in the Name of the Father, and of the Son, and of the Holy Ghost. AMEN.

*Then taking their clasped right hands in his hand, the Minister shall say:*

Forasmuch as you ———, and you ———, have consented together, after God's Holy Ordinance of Marriage; and have plighted your faith and truth to each other in the presence of God and of these witnesses; and have confirmed the same by giving and receiving a ring; now, therefore, I pronounce you husband and wife. In the Name of the Father, and of the Son, and of the Holy Ghost. AMEN.

Whom, therefore God hath joined together, let not man put asunder.

LET US PRAY.

O FAITHFUL GOD, who keepest covenant and truth with them that love Thee, hear Thou in heaven Thy dwelling-place, this marriage-vow which Thy servant and handmaid have vowed before Thee. And grant unto them the grace of Thy Good Spirit, that with all fidelity they may observe and keep it; walking together in Thy faith and fear; being led by the Angel of Thy presence, and strengthened by Thy hand, until they come to the inheritance of the saints in light: through Jesus Christ our Lord, Who has commanded us to pray, saying:

OUR FATHER WHO ART IN HEAVEN, HALLOWED BE THY NAME: THY KINGDOM COME: THY WILL BE DONE ON EARTH, AS IT IS IN HEAVEN: GIVE US THIS DAY OUR DAILY BREAD: AND FORGIVE US OUR DEBTS, AS WE FORGIVE OUR DEBTORS: AND LEAD US NOT INTO TEMPTATION, BUT DELIVER US FROM EVIL: FOR THINE IS THE KINGDOM, AND THE POWER, AND THE GLORY, FOR EVER. AMEN.

And the Minister shall pronounce over them this Benediction:

The blessing of God Almighty, the Father, the Son, and the Holy Ghost, be upon you, and remain with you always. AMEN.

# XII.

## Office for the Burial of the Dead.

On entering the church, the Minister may use the following Sentences.

Or, if all the services be performed at the house, he may begin with these Sentences.

I AM the Resurrection and the Life, saith the Lord; he that believeth in Me, though he were dead, yet shall he live: and whosoever liveth and believeth in Me, shall never die.

None of us liveth to himself, and no man dieth to himself; for whether we live, we live unto the Lord, and whether we die, we die unto the Lord: whether we live therefore or die, we are the Lord's. For to this end Christ both died and rose, and revived, that He might be Lord both of the dead and living.

We brought nothing into this world, and it is certain we can carry nothing out.

The Lord gave, and the Lord hath taken away; blessed be the Name of the Lord.

Then may be read, or chanted.

## PSALM XC.

1. LORD, Thou hast been our dwelling-place in all generations.

2. Before the mountains were brought forth, or ever Thou hadst formed the earth and the world, even from everlasting to everlasting, Thou *art* God.

3. Thou turnest man to destruction; and sayest, Return, ye children of men.

4. For a thousand years in Thy sight *are but* as yesterday when it is past, and *as* a watch in the night.

5. Thou carriest them away as with a flood; they are *as* a sleep: in the morning *they are* like grass *which* groweth up.

6. In the morning it flourisheth, and groweth up, in the evening it is cut down, and withereth.

7. For we are consumed by Thine anger, and by Thy wrath are we troubled.

8. Thou hast set our iniquities before Thee, our secret *sins* in the light of Thy countenance.

9. For all our days are passed away in Thy wrath: we spend our years as a tale *that is told*.

10. The days of our years *are* threescore years and ten; and if by reason of strength *they be* fourscore years, yet *is* their strength, labor and sorrow; for it is soon cut off, and we fly away.

11. Who knoweth the power of Thine anger? even according to Thy fear, *so is* Thy wrath.

12. So teach *us* to number our days, that we may apply *our* hearts unto wisdom.

Then the Minister shall say:

Hear the Word of God as it is written in the fifteenth chapter of St. Paul's first Epistle to the Corinthians, beginning with the thirty-fifth verse:

But some *man* will say, How are the dead raised up? and with what body do they come? *Thou* fool, that which thou sowest is not quickened except it die: And that which thou sowest, thou sowest not that body that shall be, but bare grain; it may chance of wheat, or of some other *grain:* But God giveth it a body as it hath pleased Him, and to every seed his own body. All flesh *is* not the same flesh; but *there is* one *kind of* flesh of men, another flesh-of beasts, another of fishes, and another of birds. *There are* also celestial bodies, and bodies terrestrial: but the glory of the celestial *is* one, and the *glory* of the terrestrial *is* another. *There is* one glory of the sun, and another glory of the moon, and another glory of the stars; for *one* star differeth from *another* star in glory. So also *is* the resurrection of the dead. It is sown in corruption, it is raised in incorruption; It is sown in dishonor, it is raised in glory: it is sown in weakness, it is raised in power: It is sown a natural body, it is raised a spiritual body. There is a natural body, and there is a spiritual body. And so it is written, The first man Adam was made a living soul; the last Adam *was made* a Quickening Spirit. Howbeit, that *was* not first which is spiritual, but that which is natural; and afterward that which is spiritual. The first man *is* of the earth, earthy: the second Man *is* the Lord from heaven. As *is* the earthy, such *are* they also that are earthy: and as *is* the Heavenly, such *are* they also that are heavenly. And as we have borne the image of the earthy, we shall also bear the image of the Heavenly. Now this I say, brethren, that flesh and blood cannot inherit the kingdom of God; neither doth corruption inherit incorruption.

Behold, I show you a mystery; we shall not all sleep, but we shall all be changed, in a moment, in the twinkling of an eye, at the last trump: for the trumpet shall sound, and the dead shall be raised incorruptible, and we shall be changed. For this corruptible must put on incorruption, and this mortal *must* put on immortality. So when this corruptible shall have put on incorruption, and this mortal shall have put on immortality, then shall be brought to pass the saying that is written, Death is swallowed up in victory. O death, where *is* thy sting? O grave, where *is* thy victory? The sting of death *is* sin; and the strength of sin *is* the law. But thanks *be* to God, Which giveth us the victory, through our Lord Jesus Christ. Therefore, my beloved brethren, be ye steadfast, unmovable, always abounding in the work of the Lord; forasmuch as ye know that your labor is not in vain in the Lord.

[FOR A CHILD.]

Hear the Gospel of our Saviour Jesus Christ, in reference to little children.

AND they brought young children to Him, that He should touch them; and His disciples rebuked those that brought them. But when Jesus saw it He was much displeased, and said unto them, Suffer the little children to come unto Me, and forbid them not; for of such is the kingdom of God. Verily I say unto you, Whosoever shall not receive the kingdom of God as a little child, he shall not enter therein. And He took them up in His arms, put His hands upon them, and blessed them.

Take heed that ye despise not one of these little

ones; for I say unto you, that in heaven their angels do always behold the face of My Father which is in heaven.

For the Son of Man is come to save that which was lost. How think ye? If a man have a hundred sheep, and one of them be gone astray, doth he not leave the ninety and nine, and goeth into the mountains and seeketh that which is gone astray? And if so be that he find it, verily I say unto you, he rejoiceth more of that sheep, than of the ninety and nine which went not astray. Even so, it is not the will of your Father which is in heaven, that one of these little ones should perish.

Therefore are they before the throne of God, and serve Him day and night in His temple: and He that sitteth on the throne shall dwell among them. They shall hunger no more, neither thirst any more; neither shall the sun light on them, nor any heat. For the Lamb which is in the midst of the throne shall feed them, and shall lead them unto living fountains of waters: and God shall wipe away all tears from their eyes.

The Lord gave; and the Lord hath taken away; blessed be the Name of the Lord.

After the reading of Holy Scripture the Minister shall say:

Let us pray.

ALMIGHTY AND MOST MERCIFUL GOD, the consolation of the sorrowful, and the support of the weary, Who dost not willingly grieve or afflict the children of men; look down in tender love and pity, we beseech Thee, upon Thy servants, this bereaved household, whose joy is turned into mourning; and according to the multitude of Thy mercies be pleased to uphold, strengthen, and comfort them, that they may not faint under Thy Fatherly chastening, but find in Thee their strength and refuge; through Jesus Christ our Lord. AMEN.

OUR FATHER, etc.

Then may follow an ADDRESS.

After which the Minister shall say: Let us pray.

ALMIGHTY GOD, with Whom do live the spirits of those who depart hence in the Lord, and with Whom the souls of the faithful, after they are delivered from the burden of the flesh, are in joy and felicity; we give Thee hearty thanks for the good examples of all those Thy servants, who, having finished their course in faith, do now rest from their labors. And we beseech Thee, that we, with all those who are departed in the true faith of Thy Holy Name, may have our perfect consummation and bliss, both in body and soul, in Thy eternal and everlasting glory; through Jesus Christ our Lord. AMEN.

O THOU EVER-BLESSED MEDIATOR, Who wast dead, but livest forever, of Whom the whole family in heaven and earth is named, and Who hast knit all Thy saints in one communion unto life eternal, in that mystical Body of which Thou art the glorious and ever-living Head; grant us grace so to follow Thy blessed saints, who have gone before us, in the faith and fellowship of Thy Holy Church, that we may come to those unspeakable joys, which Thou hast prepared for all that love Thee, from the foundation of the world. AMEN.

O GOD, Whose days are without end, and Whose mercies cannot be numbered; make us, we beseech Thee, deeply sensible of the shortness and uncertainty of human life; and let Thy Holy Spirit lead us through this vale of misery, in holiness and righteousness all the days of our lives: that when we shall have served Thee in our generation, we may be gathered unto our fathers, having the testimony of a good conscience; in the communion of the Christian Church; in the confidence of a certain faith; in the comfort of a reasonable, religious, and holy hope; in favor with Thee our God, and in perfect charity with the world: all which we ask through Jesus Christ our Lord. AMEN.

*Then standing near the coffin, or having reached the place of burial, the Minister will say:*

In the midst of life we are in death!
What helper shall we seek but Thee, O Lord,
Who because of our sins art justly angry!
O Holy God, Holy and Strong, Holy and Compassionate Saviour,
Give us not over to bitter death!

*Then, while the earth shall be cast upon the body by some standing by, the Minister will say:*

Forasmuch as it hath pleased Almighty God to take out of this world the soul of our departed *brother*, we therefore commit *his* body to the ground; earth to earth, ashes to ashes, dust to dust; looking for the general Resurrection in the last day, and the Life of the world to come, through our Lord Jesus Christ; at Whose second coming in glorious majesty to judge the world, the earth and the sea shall give up their dead ; and the corruptible bodies of those who sleep in Him shall be changed, and made like unto His glorious body ; according to the working whereby He is able even to subdue all things unto Himself.

I know that my Redeemer liveth, and that He shall stand at the latter day upon the earth. And though after my skin worms destroy this body, yet in my flesh shall I see God; Whom I shall see for myself, and mine eyes shall behold, and not another.

I would not have you to be ignorant, brethren, concerning them which are asleep, that ye sorrow not, even as others which have no hope. For if we believe that Jesus died and rose again, even so them also which sleep in Jesus will God bring with Him.

Let us pray.

ALMIGHTY GOD, who by the death of Thy dear Son Jesus Christ hast destroyed death ; by His rest in the tomb hast sanctified the graves of the saints; and by His glorious resurrection has brought life and immortality to light : receive, we beseech Thee our unfeigned thanks for that victory over death and the grave which He has obtained for us and for all who sleep in Him ; and keep us in everlasting fellowship with all that wait for Thee on earth, and with all that are around Thee in heaven; in union with Him who is the Resurrection and the Life; Who liveth and reigneth with Thee and the Holy Ghost, ever One God, world without end. AMEN.

ALMIGHTY GOD, our Heavenly Father, who, in Thy perfect wisdom and mercy, hast ended for Thy servants departed the voyage of this troublous life; Grant, we beseech Thee, that we who are still to continue our course amidst earthly dangers, temptations, and troubles, may evermore be protected by Thy mercy; and finally come to the haven of eternal salvation, through Jesus Christ our Lord. AMEN.

The grace of our Lord Jesus Christ, and the love of God, and the fellowship of the Holy Ghost, be with you all, evermore. AMEN.

# XIII.

## Prayers for Special Occasions.

---

### A PRAYER BEFORE THE EXPLANATION OF THE CATECHISM.

O HEAVENLY Father, Thy Word is perfect, converting the soul; a sure testimony, making wise the simple, enlightening the eyes of the blind: and a powerful means unto salvation, for all those who believe. And whereas we are not only blind by nature, but even incapable of doing any good: and also since Thou wilt help none but those who are of a broken and contrite heart; we beseech Thee to enlighten our understanding with Thy Holy Spirit, and give us a meek heart, free from all haughtiness and carnal knowledge, that we, hearing Thy Word, may rightly understand it, and regulate our life accordingly. Be graciously pleased to convert all those who still stray from Thy truth, that we may, together with them, unanimously serve Thee in true holiness and righteousness all the days of our life.

We crave all these things for Christ's sake, who

hath thus taught us to pray in His Name, and promised to hear us:

OUR FATHER WHO ART IN HEAVEN, HALLOWED BE THY NAME: THY KINGDOM COME: THY WILL BE DONE ON EARTH AS IT IS IN HEAVEN: GIVE US THIS DAY OUR DAILY BREAD: AND FORGIVE US OUR DEBTS, AS WE FORGIVE OUR DEBTORS: AND LEAD US NOT INTO TEMPTATION, BUT DELIVER US FROM EVIL: FOR THINE IS THE KINGDOM, AND THE POWER, AND THE GLORY, FOR EVER. AMEN.

A PRAYER AFTER THE EXPLANATION OF THE CATECHISM.

O GRACIOUS God and Merciful Father, we give Thee hearty thanks that it hath pleased Thee, not only to take us, but also our little children, into Thy covenant, which Thou hast not only sealed unto them, by Holy Baptism, but also daily showest, when Thou perfectest Thy praise out of their mouths, thus to cause the wise of the world to blush. We beseech Thee, increase Thy grace in them, that they may always grow and increase in Christ Thy Son; till they acquire their perfect manly age in all knowledge and righteousness. Give us grace that we may educate them, as Thou hast commanded us, in Thy knowledge and fear, so that by their godliness the kingdom of Satan may be destroyed, and the Kingdom of Jesus Christ strengthened in this and other congregations, to the glory of Thy Holy Name, and to their eternal salvation, through Jesus Christ. AMEN.

A PRAYER AT THE OPENING OF THE CONSISTORY.

HEAVENLY FATHER, Eternal and Merciful God, it hath pleased Thee of Thy infinite wisdom and goodness to gather a Church to Thyself out of all nations upon the face of the earth, by the preaching of Thy Holy Gospel, and to govern the same by the service of men. Thou hast also graciously called us up to this office, and commanded us to take heed unto ourselves and unto the flock, which Christ hath bought with His precious blood. Since we are at this present assembled in Thy Holy Name, after the example of the Apostolic Churches, to consult, as our office requires, about those things which may come before us, for the welfare and edification of Thy Church, for which we acknowledge ourselves to be unfit and incapable, as we are by nature unable of ourselves to think any good, much less to put it in practice: therefore, we beseech Thee, O Faithful God and Father, that Thou wilt be pleased to be present with Thy Holy Spirit, according to Thy promise, in the midst of our present assembly, to guide us in all truth. Remove from us all misapprehensions and unbecoming desires of the flesh, and grant that Thy Holy Word may be the only rule and guide of all our consultations; that they may tend to the glory of Thy Name, to the edification of Thy Church, and to the discharge of our own consciences, through Jesus Christ Thy Son, who with Thee and the Holy Ghost, the Only True God, is eternally to be praised and magnified. AMEN.

A PRAYER AT THE CLOSE OF THE CONSISTORY.

O Lord God and Heavenly Father, we heartily thank Thee, that Thou hast been pleased to gather a Church to Thyself in this part of the world, and to use our service therein, granting us the privilege that we may freely and without hindrance preach Thy Holy Gospel, and exercise all the duties of godliness: moreover, we thank Thee, that Thou now hast been present with Thy Holy Spirit in the midst of this our assembly, directing our determinations according to Thy will, uniting our hearts in mutual peace and concord—We beseech Thee, O Faithful God and Father, that Thou wilt graciously be pleased to bless our intended labor, and effectually to execute Thy begun work, always gathering unto Thyself a true Church, and preserving the same in the pure doctrine, and in the right use of Thy Holy Sacraments, and in a diligent exercise of discipline. On the contrary, destroy all evil and crafty counsels, which are devised against Thy Word and Church. Strengthen also all the Ministers of Thy Church, that they may faithfully and steadfastly declare Thy Holy Word: and the Magistrates of Thy people, that they may bear the sword with righteousness and discretion. Particularly we pray for those whom Thou hast been pleased to put in authority over us. Grant that their whole government may be thus directed, that the King of all kings may rule over them and their fellow-citizens; and that the kingdom of the devil (which is a kingdom of scandal and reproach) may, daily more and more be destroyed and brought to naught by them as Thy servants, and that we may lead with them a quiet and peaceable life, in all godliness and honesty. Hear us, O God and Father, through Jesus Christ Thy Beloved Son, Who with Thee and the Holy Ghost the Only and True God, is eternally to be magnified and praised. AMEN.

A PRAYER AT THE MEETING OF THE DEACONS.

MERCIFUL GOD and Father, Thou hast not only said unto us that we should always have the poor with us, but hast also commanded that they should be assisted; and for that end hast ordained the service of Deacons in Thy Church, by whom they might be relieved. As we, who are called to the office of Deacons in this congregation, are here at present met in Thy Name, to consult together concerning our ministry; therefore we humbly beseech Thee, for the sake of Jesus Christ, that Thou wilt be pleased to endue us with the spirit of discretion; to the end that we may rightly discern who are really poor and who are not: and that we may, with all cheerfulness and fidelity, distribute the alms collected by us to every one according to his necessity; not leaving the indigent members of Thy Beloved Son comfortless, neither giving to those who are not in want. Kindle within the hearts of men an ardent love towards the poor, that they may liberally give of their temporal goods, of which Thou hast made them stewards: and that we, having the means in hand to assist the indigent, may faithfully, without vexation, and with a free heart, perform our office. Grant us the talents, to comfort the miserable, not only with the external gift, but also with the Holy Word. And since man doth not live by bread alone, but by every word that proceedeth out of Thy mouth, be pleased therefore to extend Thy blessing over our distributions, and increase the bread of the poor, that both we and they may have reason to praise and thank Thee: expecting the blessed coming of Thy Beloved Son Jesus Christ, Who became poor for our sakes, to make us rich in eternity. AMEN.

### EUCHARISTIC PRAYER.

The Constitution of the Church directs that in the administration of the Lord's Supper, "after the sermon and usual prayers are ended, the Form for the administration of the Lord's Supper shall be read, and a prayer suited to the occasion shall be offered, before the members participate of the ordinance."

The following is submitted as a suitable prayer, which may be used in compliance with this direction.

IT is very meet and right, above all things, to give thanks unto Thee, O Eternal God: Who, by Thy word, didst create heaven and earth, and all things therein. For all Thy bounties known to us, for all unknown, we give Thee thanks; but chiefly, that when, through disobedience, we had fallen from Thee, Thou didst not suffer us to depart from Thee forever, but hast ransomed us from eternal death, and given us the joyful hope of everlasting life, through Jesus Christ Thy Son; Who, being Very and Eternal God, became Man for us men, and for our salvation.

Not as we ought, but as we are able, we bless Thee for His holy incarnation; for His life on earth; for His precious sufferings and death upon the cross; for His resurrection from the dead; and for His glorious ascension to Thy right hand.

We bless Thee for the giving of the Holy Ghost; for the sacraments and ordinances of the Church; for the communion of Christ's Body and Blood; for the great hope of everlasting life, and of an eternal weight of glory.

Thee, Mighty God, Heavenly King, we magnify and praise. With angels and archangels, and all the hosts of heaven, we worship and adore Thy glorious Name, joining in the song of Cherubim and Seraphim, and saying:—

HOLY, HOLY, HOLY, LORD GOD OF SABAOTH, HEAVEN AND EARTH ARE FULL OF THY GLORY. HOSANNA IN THE HIGHEST. BLESSED IS HE THAT COMETH IN THE NAME OF THE LORD. HOSANNA IN THE HIGHEST.

And we most humbly beseech Thee, O Merciful Father, to vouchsafe unto us Thy gracious presence, as we commemorate in this Supper the most blessed sacrifice of Thy Son; and to bless and sanctify with Thy Word and Spirit these Thine own gifts of bread and wine which we set before Thee; that we, receiving them, according to our Saviour's institution, in thankful remembrance of His death and passion, may, through the power of the Holy Ghost, be very partakers of His body and blood, with all His benefits, to our salvation and the glory of Thy Most Holy Name.

And here we offer and present to Thee, O Lord, ourselves, our souls and bodies, to be a reasonable, holy, and living sacrifice unto Thee; humbly beseeching Thee that all who are partakers of this Holy Communion, may be filled with Thy grace and heavenly benediction. And although we be unworthy, through our manifold sins, to offer unto Thee any sacrifice, yet we beseech Thee to accept this our bounden duty and service; not weighing our merits, but pardoning our offences, through Jesus Christ our Lord.

And rejoicing in the communion of Thy saints, we bless Thy Holy Name for all Thy servants who have departed in the faith, and who, having accomplished their warfare, are at rest with Thee; beseeching Thee to enable us so to follow their faith and good example, that we with them may finally be partakers of Thy heavenly Kingdom—when, made like unto Christ, we shall behold Him with unveiled face, rejoicing in His glory, and by Him we, with all Thy Church, holy and unspotted, shall be presented with exceeding joy before the presence of Thy glory. Hear us, O Heavenly Father, for His sake: to Whom, with Thee and the Holy Ghost, be glory for ever and ever.

AMEN.

### A MORNING PRAYER.

O MERCIFUL Father, we thank Thee, that Thou hast in faithfulness watched over us the night past: and we beseech Thee to strengthen, and henceforth guide us by Thy Holy Spirit, that we may spend this, and all the days of our lives, in all righteousness and holiness; and that whatsoever we undertake, we may always aim at the promoting of Thy glory, and expect all the success of our undertakings from Thy bountiful hand alone. And to the end that we may obtain this mercy of Thee, be pleased (according to Thy promise) to forgive all our sins, through the holy passion and blood-shedding of our Lord and Saviour Jesus Christ; for we heartily repent of them. Enlighten also our hearts, that we, having cast off all works of darkness, may, as children of light, walk in a new life in all godliness. Bless also the preaching of Thy Gospel. Destroy all the works of the devil. Strengthen all ministers of the Gospel and magistrates of thy people. Comfort all those who are persecuted and afflicted in mind; through Jesus Christ Thy Beloved Son, Who hath promised us that Thou wilt certainly give us whatsoever we shall ask in His Name, and therefore hath commanded us to pray: OUR FATHER, etc.

### AN EVENING PRAYER.

O MERCIFUL God, Eternal Light, shining in darkness, Thou who dispellest the night of sin, and all blindness of heart; since Thou hast appointed the night for rest and the day for labour, we beseech Thee, grant that our bodies may rest in peace and quietness, that afterwards they may be able to endure the labour they must bear. Temper our sleep, that it be not disorderly, that we may remain spotless both in body and soul, nay, that our sleep itself may be to Thy glory. Enlighten the eyes of our understanding, that we may not sleep in death; but always look for deliverance from this misery. Defend us against all assaults of the devil, and take us into Thy holy protection. And although we have not passed this day without having greatly sinned against Thee, we beseech Thee to hide our sins with Thy great mercy, as thou hidest all things on earth with the darkness of the night, that we therefore may not be cast out from Thy presence. Relieve and comfort all those who are afflicted or distressed in mind, body, or estate; through Jesus Christ our Lord, Who hath taught us to pray; OUR FATHER, etc.

A PRAYER FOR THE PRESIDENT OF THE UNITED STATES AND ALL IN AUTHORITY.

O LORD, our Heavenly Father, the High and Mighty Ruler of the Universe, who dost from Thy throne behold all the dwellers upon earth; most heartily we beseech Thee, with Thy favor to behold and bless Thy servant, THE PRESIDENT OF THE UNITED STATES, and all others in authority; and so replenish them with the grace of thy Holy Spirit, that they may always incline to Thy will, and walk in Thy way. Endue them plenteously with heavenly gifts; grant them in health and prosperity long to live; and finally, after this life, to attain everlasting joy and felicity; through Jesus Christ our Lord. AMEN.

A PRAYER FOR ALL CONDITIONS OF MEN.

O GOD, the Creator and Preserver of all mankind, we humbly beseech Thee for all sorts and conditions of men; that Thou wouldest be pleased to make Thy ways known unto them, Thy saving health unto all nations. More especially we pray for Thy Holy Church Universal; that it may be so guided and governed by Thy Good Spirit, that all who profess and call themselves Christians may be led into the way of truth, and hold the faith in unity of spirit, in the bond of peace, and in righteousness of life. Finally, we commend to Thy fatherly goodness all those who are any ways afflicted, or distressed, in mind, body, or estate; that it may please Thee to comfort and relieve them, according to their several necessities; giving them patience under their sufferings, and a happy issue out of all their afflictions. And this we beg for Jesus Christ's sake. AMEN.

### THANKSGIVING AFTER HARVEST.

WE yield Thee hearty thanks, most merciful Father, for all Thy goodness, and especially for this Thy bounty again bestowed upon us, who, through Thy providence and tender mercy towards us, have now reaped the fruits of the earth in due season, and gathered them into our garners. Continue, we beseech Thee, Thy loving-kindness towards us, that year by year our land may yield her increase, filling our hearts with food and gladness, to the comfort of Thy people and the glory of Thy Holy Name; and so dispose us by Thy special grace preventing us, that we Thy servants may never sow only to the flesh, lest of the flesh we reap corruption, but may sow spiritually to life everlasting, and reap the same in Thy heavenly kingdom; through Jesus Christ our Lord. AMEN.

### A GENERAL THANKSGIVING.

ALMIGHTY God, Father of all mercies, we, Thine unworthy servants, do give Thee most humble and hearty thanks for all Thy goodness and loving-kindness to us, and to all men. We bless Thee for our creation, preservation, and all the blessings of this life; but above all, for Thine inestimable love in the redemption of the world by our Lord Jesus Christ; for the means of grace and for the hope of glory. And, we beseech Thee, give us that due sense of all Thy mercies, that our hearts may be unfeignedly thankful, and that we may show forth Thy praise, not only with our lips, but in our lives; by giving up ourselves to Thy service, and by walking before Thee in holiness and righteousness all our days; through Jesus Christ our Lord, to Whom, with Thee and the Holy Ghost, be all honor and glory, world without end. AMEN.

### A PRAYER IN TIME OF DROUGHT.

O GOD, our Creator, Preserver, and Bountiful Benefactor, Who givest seed-time and harvest, and sendest both the early and latter rain; have pity, we beseech Thee, upon Thy famished people who cry unto Thee in their tribulation, and in Thy compassion return and visit us; that the heavens may no longer be as brass above, and the earth as iron beneath, to shut out from us Thy mercy; but that all the people may praise Thee, O God, Who art the Fountain of living waters and the Father of mercies, from Whom cometh down every good and perfect gift; through Jesus Christ our Lord. AMEN.

### A PRAYER IN TIME OF PESTILENCE.

HOLY Lord God Almighty, Who of old didst stay the Angel of Pestilence at the cry of Thy repenting children, and bring back health to a dying people; hear us, Thy suppliants, returning to Thee, as in sackcloth, dust and ashes, and mercifully lift from us the heavy hand of Thy righteous visitation; that the people may live before Thee, and not die in their sins, and that the land may no longer mourn by reason of Thy judgments, O Lord, Who for our iniquities art justly displeased. We ask it humbly in the Name of our Lord Jesus Christ. AMEN.

### FOR FAIR WEATHER.

O GOD of love and compassion, Who of old didst set Thy bow in the cloud for a token of a covenant between Thee and the earth, we humble ourselves before thee on account of our sins, and acknowledge Thy chastisement to be just. Yet spare us, O Lord. Stay the excess of rain, and cause Thy sun to shine, that, the hope of harvest being fulfilled, our barns may be stored with Thy bounty, and our souls rejoice in Thee. Above all, O Lord, grant that the Sun of Righteousness may arise upon us with healing in his wings, and Thy people, walking all the day in the light of Thy countenance, in thy right eousness may be exalted. Do this, O Father of Mercies, for the sake of Thy Son Jesus Christ. AMEN.

### FOR PEACE.

O God of Peace, Who didst send unto us messages of peace by thy Son, the Prince of Peace, and commandest us to be at peace with all men, we entreat Thee to save us from quarrel, bloodshed, and war. Still the tumult of the people as Thou dost the raging of the sea.* Disappoint the devices of the wicked, and bring their machinations to naught. Fill our hearts and the hearts of all men with Thy love, so that we may dwell in safety under the wings of Thy Holy Spirit, and have peace with God through Our Lord Jesus Christ. AMEN.

### FOR THE ABSENT FROM HOME.

O GOD, Who art everywhere present, ruling the sea and the land, we entreat Thee for Thy *servant* now absent from us. Rescue *him* from peril, from sickness, from sin, and from death. Cover *him* as with a shield, and sanctify *his* experience of Thy mercy to *his* eternal profit and joy. In due time restore *him* to *his* home, and keep *him* and us through the journey of this life, that we may all reach our Father's house in peace, through His grace Who hath opened the kingdom of Heaven to all who believe in His Holy Name. AMEN.

---

\* In time of war may be here inserted:

Give us not over into the hands of our enemies, but defend us and grant us the victory, which is in Thine hand.

## ON COMMENCING A JOURNEY.

O MOST Glorious Lord God, Who of old didst lead Thine armies as with a pillar of cloud by day and of fire by night, be our Leader and Guardian, we beseech Thee, in all our journeyings; our support in setting out; our solace on the way; our shadow in the heat; our covert in the rain and cold; the help of our weariness; the fortress of our adversity; and our staff in the way of danger; that under Thy guidance we may safely come to our journey's end, and at length to the end of this our earthly warfare and pilgrimage; through Jesus Christ our Lord. AMEN.

## FOR A PERSON GOING TO SEA.

O ETERNAL Lord God, Who alone spreadest out the heavens, and rulest the raging of the sea: We commend to Thine Almighty protection Thy *servant*, for whose preservation on the great deep our prayers are desired. Guard *him*, we beseech Thee, from the dangers of the sea, from sickness, from the violence of enemies, from every evil; and conduct *him* in safety to the haven where *he* would be, with a grateful sense of Thy mercies: through Jesus Christ our Lord. AMEN.

## FOR THE SICK.

O LORD God, in Whose hand our breath is; regard with tender compassion Thy servant, whom it hath pleased Thee to visit with sickness. Be graciously near to *him* in the hour of *his* need. Grant unto *him* true repentance for all *his* sins, a firm and steady trust in the merits of Thy Son, Jesus Christ, and grace to be in perfect charity with all men. Enable *him* to cast all *his* cares on Thee, and to yield *himself* with childlike submission to Thy righteous will.

GOD of all power and grace, bless, we entreat Thee, the means used for *his* recovery, rebuke the violence of disease, and raise *him* up from *his* bed of pain, that, being delivered by Thy compassion, *he* may walk before Thee in newness of life. But if, O Most Wise and Merciful Father, this sickness should be unto death, grant *him*, we humbly implore Thee, a comfortable release from all *his* sufferings. Let the arms of Thine everlasting love be around *him*, and, when flesh and heart shall fail, be Thou the strength of *his* heart and *his* portion for evermore: through the mediation and merits of Thy Son, Jesus Christ, our Lord. AMEN.

### FOR A SICK CHILD.

O ALMIGHTY God and Merciful Father, to Whom alone belong the issues of life and death; look down from Heaven, we humbly beseech Thee, upon this child, now lying upon the bed of sickness. Visit *him*, O Lord, with Thy salvation, deliver *him* in Thy good time from his bodily pain, and save *his* soul for Thy mercies' sake; that if it shall be Thy pleasure to prolong *his* days here on earth, *he* may live to Thee, and be an instrument of Thy glory, by serving Thee faithfully, and doing good in *his* generation; or else receive *him* into those heavenly habitations, where the souls of those who sleep in the Lord Jesus enjoy perpetual rest and felicity. Grant this, O Lord, for Thy mercies' sake, in the Name of Thy Son, Our Lord Jesus Christ, who liveth, and reigneth with Thee and the Holy Ghost, ever one God, world without end. AMEN.

### FOR GRACE TO USE ARIGHT THE WORD.

BLESSED LORD, Who hast caused all Holy Scriptures to be written for our learning; grant that we may in such wise hear them, read, mark, learn, and inwardly digest them, that by patience and comfort of Thy Holy Word we may embrace and ever hold fast the blessed hope of everlasting life which Thou hast given us in our Savour Jesus Christ. AMEN.

### FOR FORGIVENESS.

ALMIGHTY and Everlasting God, Who hatest nothing that Thou hast made, and dost forgive the sins of all those who are penitent; Create and make in us new and contrite hearts, that we, worthily lamenting our sins, and acknowledging our wretchedness, may obtain of Thee, the God of all mercy, perfect remission and forgiveness; through Jesus Christ our Lord. AMEN.

### FOR PROTECTION.

ALMIGHTY God, Who seest that we have no power of ourselves to help ourselves: Keep us both outwardly in our bodies and inwardly in our souls; that we may be defended from all adversities which may happen to the body, and from all evil thoughts which may assault and hurt the soul; and as we have received how we ought to walk and please Thee, so may we abound more and more; through our Lord and Saviour Jesus Christ. AMEN.

### AT THE CHRISTMAS SEASON.

ALMIGHTY God, give us grace that we may cast away the works of darkness, and put upon us the armor of light, now in the time of this mortal life, in which Thy Son Jesus Christ came to visit us with great humility: that in the last day, when He shall come again in His glorious Majesty to judge both the quick and dead, we may rise to the life immortal: through Him who liveth and reigneth with Thee and the Holy Ghost, now and ever. AMEN.

O LORD, Who hast given us cause of perpetual joy by the coming of Thy Son our Saviour among us: Raise up Thy power, we pray Thee, and possess us with a mighty sense of Thy wonderful love; that whereas through the cares of this life we are sorely let and hindered in running the race that is set before us, we may be careful for nothing, but thankfully commending ourselves in everything to Thy bountiful grace and mercy, the peace of Thee, our God, which passeth all understanding, may keep our hearts and minds, through the satisfaction of Thy Son our Lord; to Whom, with Thee and the Holy Ghost, be honor and glory, world without end. AMEN.

## AT THE EASTER SEASON.

ALMIGHTY GOD, Who hast given Thine Only Son to be unto us both a sacrifice for sin, and also an example of godly life: Give us grace that we may always most thankfully receive that His most inestimable benefit; and also daily endeavor to follow the blessed steps of His most holy life; that dying unto sin, and living unto righteousness, we may at last obtain eternal life: Through the same Jesus Christ our Lord. AMEN.

BLESSED Lord, Whose Only Son our Saviour Jesus Christ, hath once suffered for our sins, the just for the unjust, that He might bring us to Thee our God: We beseech Thee, that as we are baptized into His death, so by continually mortifying our corrupt affections we may be buried with Him; and at last through the grave, and gate of death, pass to our joyful resurrection: For His merits, Who died, and was buried, and rose again, Thy Son Jesus Christ our Lord. AMEN.

ALMIGHTY and Everlasting God, Who of Thy tender love towards mankind has sent Thy Son, our Saviour Jesus Christ, to take upon Him our flesh, and that in the form of a servant, and to suffer death, even the death of the Cross, for our redemption, and that we should follow the example of His great humility, patience, and obedience: Mercifully grant that this mind may be in us which was also in Christ Jesus, that we may both follow the example of His humble obedience and patient suffering, and also be made partakers of His glorious resurrection, to live with Thee for ever. Grant this for the sake of Thy Son our Saviour Jesus Christ. AMEN.

### AT THE SEASON OF PENTECOST.

O GOD the King of Glory, Who hast exalted Thine Only Son Jesus Christ with great triumph unto Thy Kingdom in heaven; We beseech Thee, leave us not comfortless; but send to us Thy Holy Ghost to comfort us, and exalt us unto the same place whither our Saviour Christ is gone before; Who liveth and reigneth with Thee and the Holy Ghost, One God, world without end. AMEN.

God of all peace and consolation, Who didst gloriously fulfil the great promise of the Gospel, by sending down Thy Holy Ghost on the day of Pentecost, to establish the Church as the home of His continual presence and power among men; mercifully grant unto us, we beseech Thee, this same gift of the Spirit, to renew, illuminate, refresh, and sanctify our dying souls, to be over us and around us like the light and dew of heaven, and to be in us evermore as a well of water springing up into everlasting life; through Jesus Christ our Lord, to Whom, with Thee, and the Holy Ghost, ever One God, be honor and glory, world without end. AMEN.

# XIV.

## The Creeds.

### THE APOSTLES' CREED.

I BELIEVE in God the Father Almighty, Maker of heaven and earth;

And in Jesus Christ, His Only Son our Lord; Who was conceived by the Holy Ghost, born of the Virgin Mary, suffered under Pontius Pilate, was crucified, dead, and buried; He descended into hell; the third day He rose again from the dead; He ascended into heaven, and sitteth on the right hand of God the Father Almighty; from thence he shall come to judge the quick and the dead.

I believe in the Holy Ghost; the Holy Catholic Church,. the communion of saints; the forgiveness of sins; the resurrection of the body; and the life everlasting. AMEN.

### THE CONFESSION OF FAITH,
#### COMPOSED IN THE COUNCIL OF NICE, A. D., 325.

WE believe in one God, the Father Almighty, Maker of heaven and earth, and of all things visible and invisible;

And in one Lord Jesus Christ, the Only Begotten Son of God, begotten of his Father, before all worlds; God, of God, Light, of Light, very God, of very God; begotten, not made, being of one substance with the Father, by Whom all things were made: Who, for us men and for our salvation, came down from heaven, and was incarnate by the Holy Ghost of the Virgin Mary; and was made Man; and was crucified also for us under Pontius Pilate. He suffered and was buried; and the third day He arose again according to the Scriptures; and ascended into heaven, and sitteth on the right hand of the Father. And He shall come again, with glory, to judge both the quick and the dead; Whose kingdom shall have no end.

And in the Holy Ghost, Who spake by the prophets. And one holy Catholic and Apostolic Church. We acknowledge one baptism for the remission of sins; and we look for the resurrection of the dead, and the life of the world to come. AMEN.

### THE CREED OF ATHANASIUS, A. D. 333.

1. WHOSOEVER will be saved, before all things it is necessary that he hold the Catholic faith.

2. Which faith, except one do keep whole and undefiled, without doubt he shall perish everlastingly.

3. The Catholic faith is this, that we worship one God in Trinity, and Trinity in Unity;

4. Neither confounding the Persons nor dividing the substance.

5. For there is one person of the Father, another of the Son, and another of the Holy Ghost.

6. But the Godhead of the Father, of the Son, and of the Holy Ghost is all one; the Glory equal, and the Majesty coeternal.

7. Such as the Father is, such is the Son, and such is the Holy Ghost.

8. The Father uncreated, the Son uncreated, and the Holy Ghost uncreated.

9 The Father incomprehensible, and the Son incomprehensible, and the Holy Ghost incomprehensible.

10. The Father eternal, the Son eternal, and the Holy Ghost eternal:

11. And yet they are not three Eternals; but one Eternal.

12. As also there are not three Incomprehensisbles, nor three Uncreated; but one Uncreated, and one Incomprehensible.

13. So likewise the Father is Almighty, the Son Almighty, and the Holy Ghost Almighty.

14. And yet they are not three Almighties, but one Almighty.

15. So the Father is God, the Son is God, and the Holy Ghost is God.

16. And yet there are not three Gods, but one God.

17. So likewise the Father is Lord, the son Lord, and the Holy Ghost Lord.

18. And yet they are not three Lords, but one Lord.

19. For, as we are compelled by the Christian truth to acknowledge each Person by Himself to be God and Lord.

20. So we are forbidden by the Catholic faith, to say, there be three Gods, or three Lords.

21. The Father is made of none, neither created nor begotten.

22. The Son is of the Father alone, not made, nor created, but begotten.

23. The Holy Ghost is of the Father, and of the Son, neither made, nor created, nor begotten, but proceeding.

24. So there is one Father, not three Fathers; one Son, not three Sons; one Holy Ghost, not three Holy Ghosts:

25. And in this Trinity, there is not first nor last.

26. But the whole three Persons are coeternal together, and coequal.

27. So that in all things, as it is aforesaid, the Unity in Trinity, and Trinity in Unity is to be worshipped.

28. He therefore that will be saved, must thus think of the Trinity.

29. Furthermore, it is necessary to everlasting salvation, that he also believe rightly the Incarnation of our Lord Jesus Christ.

30. For the right faith is, that we believe and confess, that our Lord Jesus Christ, the Son of God, is God and Man:

31. God of the substance of the Father, begotten before the world; and Man of the Substance of his Mother, born in time:

32. Perfect God and perfect Man. having a reasonable Soul and a human Body:

33. Equal to the Father, according to his God-

head: and inferior to the Father as to his Manhood:

34. Who, although He be God and Man, yet He is not two but one Christ:

35. One, not by conversion of the Godhead into flesh, but by taking of the Manhood into God.

36. He is not one by mixture of Substance, but by unity of Person.

37. For the reasonable soul and flesh is one Man; so God and Man is one Christ:

38. Who suffered for our salvation, descended into hell, rose again the third day from the dead;

39. He ascended into heaven, sits at the right hand of God, the Father Almighty:

40. From whence He shall come to judge the quick and the dead.

41. At Whose coming all men shall rise again with their bodies;

42. And shall give account for their own works.

43. And they that have done good shall go into life everlasting; and they that have done evil, into everlasting fire.

44. This is the Catholic Faith, which except a man believe faithfully, he cannot be saved.

www.ingramcontent.com/pod-product-compliance
Lightning Source LLC
Chambersburg PA
CBHW022138160426
43197CB00009B/1339